Education in Developing Asia

Volume 4

Equity and Access to Education:

Themes, Tensions, and Policies

W.O. Lee

Asian Development Bank
Comparative Education Research Centre
The University of Hong Kong

© 2004 Asian Development Bank

Jointly published by:

Asian Development Bank
6 ADB Avenue
Mandaluyong City
P.O. Box 789
0980 Manila
Philippines

Fax: (632) 636 2444
E-mail: adbpub@adb.org

and

Comparative Education Research Centre
The University of Hong Kong
Pokfulam Road
Hong Kong, China

Fax: (852) 2517 4737
E-mail: cerc@hkusub.hku.hk

Obtainable from either address.

Series: Education in Developing Asia
Series editor: Mark Bray

Layout and index by Sara Wong.

A summary of an earlier version of this booklet was presented as an article in Vol.29, No.7 (1998) of the *International Journal of Educational Research*, published by Pergamon Press. The publishers of this booklet thank Pergamon Press for permission to reproduce some of the materials from the journal article.

ISBN 971-561-532-5
ADB Publication Stock No. 010504

The series

Education in Developing Asia

has five volumes:

1. Don Adams: *Education and National Development: Priorities, Policies, and Planning*;
2. David Chapman: *Management and Efficiency in Education: Goals and Strategies*;
3. Mark Bray: *The Costs and Financing of Education: Trends and Policy Implications*;
4. W.O. Lee: *Equity and Access to Education: Themes, Tensions, and Policies*; and
5. David Chapman and Don Adams: *The Quality of Education: Dimensions and Strategies.*

Series Editor:

Mark Bray

Contents

List of Tables

List of Figures

List of Boxes

List of Abbreviations

ADB	—	Asian Development Bank
ASEAN	—	Association of Southeast Asian Nations
CIS	—	Commonwealth of Independent States
CPM	—	Capability Poverty Measure
DMC	—	Developing Member Country
GCE	—	General Certificate of Education
GDI	—	Gender-related Development Index
GDP	—	Gross Domestic Product
GEM	—	Gender Empowerment Measure
GER	—	Gross Enrollment Rate
GNP	—	Gross National Product
HDI	—	Human Development Index
HPAE	—	High-Performing Asian Economy
HPI	—	Human Poverty Index
Lao PDR	—	Lao People's Democratic Republic
NCR	—	National Capital Region
NER	—	Net Enrollment Rate
NGO	—	Nongovernment Organization
NIE	—	Newly Industrialized Economy
OECD	—	Organisation for Economic Co-operation and Development
PRC	—	People's Republic of China
PROAP	—	Principal Regional Office for Asia and the Pacific (UNESCO)
UNDP	—	United Nations Development Programme
UNESCO	—	United Nations Educational, Scientific and Cultural Organization
WCEFA	—	World Conference on Education for All

Currency Equivalents
(As of 15 March 2000)

	Currency Unit	
Dong (D)	D1.00 = $0.00007111	$1.00 = D14,063.00
Hong Kong dollar (HK$)	HK$1.00 = $0.1286	$1.00 = HK$7.778
Kip (KN)	KN1.00 = $0.0001299	$1.00 = KN7700.77
Nepalese Rupee (NRe/NRs)	NRe1.00 = $0.01454	$1.00 = NRs68.7800
Peso (P)	P1.00 = $0.02441	$1.00 = P40.9601
Yuan (Y)	Y1.00 = $0.1208	$1.00 = Y8.2789

Note

In this booklet, "$" refers to US dollars, unless otherwise specified.

Glossary

Human Development Index	One simple composite index to measure the average achievements in basic human deveploppment capabilities by using three indicators: life expectancy, education attainment, and income.
Gender-related Development Index	One simple composite index to measure gender inequality in human development.
Human Poverty Index	An index to measure deprivations in the three indicators of human life: life expectancy, education attainment, and income.
Gender Empowerment Measure	A composite measurement reflecting the relative empowerment of women and men in the political and economic sphere of activity.
Gini Index	An index to measure the extent to which the distribution of income (or, in some cases, expenditures) among individuals or households within an economy deviates from a perfectly equal distribution.
Gross Enrollment Rate	Total enrollment of a level of education, regardless of age, expressed as a percentage of the population age group corresponding to the national regulations for that level of education.

Foreword

The Asian Development Bank (ADB) is a major source of funds and technical advice for the education sector in the Asian and Pacific region. ADB has provided nearly $3.5 billion for education since 1990, representing an average of about 6 percent of total ADB lending per year during that period. ADB recognizes that human development is the basis for national and economic development, and that education – particularly basic education – is a fundamental element of human development. ADB seeks to ensure that its education investment is effectively targeted and efficiently utilized. It further recognizes that a clear policy framework based on careful analysis of the status and development needs of the education sector is necessary for effective investment.

ADB has therefore committed itself to a comprehensive process of review and analysis as the basis for preparing a new education sector policy paper. The policy paper will guide ADB in its support for education in the first years of the 21st century. It will be based on a series of activities, all designed to ensure that the education policy adequately reflects the rapidly evolving circumstances of the region.

ADB commissioned eight country case studies and five technical working papers as inputs to the policy formulation process. The case studies, undertaken by leading education research institutes in the countries concerned, analyzed the issues in education and the policies that had been developed to address the issues. The technical working papers examined selected cross-cutting issues in education development in the region. The case studies and the technical working papers were discussed at a major regional seminar involving representatives of government ministries of education, finance, and planning. Later, the case studies and working papers were integrated into a single publication *Education and National Development in Asia: Trends, Issues, Policies, and Strategies*. This study in turn was an input into ADB's education sector policy paper.

The five technical working papers contain a great deal of useful data and analysis, and it is important to ensure that they are fully available to education policymakers, practitioners, and scholars in the region and elsewhere. Consequently, revised versions are being published separately in their entirety jointly by ADB and the Comparative Education Research Centre of the University of Hong Kong as part of this series entitled *Education in Developing Asia*. ADB hopes that the papers and their wider availability will contribute to a better understanding of the emerging challenges of education development in the region. ADB is pleased to have the partnership of a well-known academic institution in this publication, and thanks the authors and their associates for their contribution.

Nihal Amerasinghe
Director
Agriculture and Social Sectors
Department (East)
Asian Development Bank

Akira Seki
Director
Agriculture and Social Sectors
Department (West)
Asian Development Bank

Introduction

Economic growth in Asia over the last three decades has been very striking. According to a 1993 World Bank report, between 1965 and 1990 the 23 economies of East Asia grew faster than all other regions in the world. And within East Asia, the eight high-performing Asian economies (HPAEs) – Japan; the four newly industrialized economies (NIEs) of Hong Kong, China; Republic of Korea; Singapore; and Taipei, China – plus Indonesia, Malaysia, and Thailand, achieved growth more than twice as fast as the other regions of the world, about three times faster than Latin America and South Asia, and five times faster than Sub-Saharan Africa.

However, this comparison has already underscored variations of growth within Asia. As Figure 1 shows, if the HPAEs are excluded from East Asia, the growth rate in East Asia would not be so impressive. Moreover, the annual growth of gross national product (GNP) per capita in South Asia was only 1.7 percent between 1965 and 1990. Thus, despite general improvement in Asia's economic development, reports on the region are full of cautious notes.

Figure 1: Average Annual Growth of Gross National Product per Capita, 1965-1990
(percent)

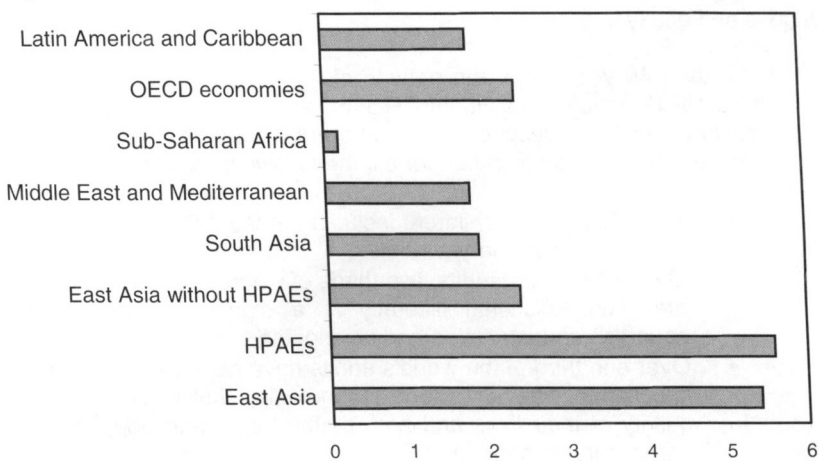

HPAEs = High-Performing Asian Economies.
OECD = Organisation for Economic Co-operation and Development.

Source: World Bank 1993, 2.

A 1997 Asian Development Bank (ADB) report on the changes and challenges in emerging Asia remarked (p.268) that:

> Life in Asia has changed remarkably during the last 30 years, and mostly for the better. On average, all standard indicators of the quality of life, such as poverty and mortality rates, have improved sharply.... [However] these changes have not been uniform.

The report added (p.268) that:

> More striking than the improvements in Asia's quality of life are the region's disparities. Differences between countries, between regions within countries, between rural and urban areas, between ethnic groups, and between the sexes are large. In many instances they have increased during the last 30 years. Life expectancy and other indicators of health and nutrition, for instance, were already higher in East Asia than South Asia in the early 1960s. Although they have improved in both subregions, East Asia has achieved more. Hence on many counts human well-being within Asia is divergent rather than converging. Within many countries the story is similar: the situation in many parts of the inland provinces of the People's Republic of China is less favorable than in the coastal provinces. In South Asia especially, women's well-being lags far behind that of men.

The report's observations match those of many other documents. The 1990 Jomtien Declaration of the World Conference on Education for All (WCEFA) commenced its preamble by highlighting the failure to achieve access and equity in education:

> More than 40 years ago, the nations of the world, speaking through the Universal Declaration of Human Rights, asserted that "everyone has a right to education." Despite notable efforts by countries around the globe to ensure the right to education for all, the following realities persist:
>
> - Over 100 million children, including at least 60 million girls, have no access to primary schooling;
> - Over 960 million adults, two thirds of whom are women, are illiterate, and functional illiteracy is a significant problem in all countries, industrialized and developing;
> - Over one third of the world's adults have no access to the printed knowledge, new skills, and technologies that could improve the quality of their lives and help them shape, and adapt to, social and cultural change; and
> - Over 100 million children and countless adults fail to complete basic education programs; millions more satisfy the attendance requirements but do not acquire essential knowledge and skills.

At the same time, the world faces daunting problems: mounting debt burdens, the threat of economic stagnation and decline, rapid population growth, widening economic disparities among and within nations, war, civil strife, violent crime, the preventable deaths of millions of children, and environmental degradation. These problems constrain efforts to meet basic learning needs. The lack of basic education among a significant proportion of the population prevents societies from addressing such problems with strength and purpose.

The *Human Development Report 1997* produced by the United Nations Development Programme (UNDP) pointed out (pp.2-3, 38-9) that the progress in reducing poverty over the 20th century had been outstanding and unprecedented, but that the advances had been uneven and marred by setbacks. The report specifically highlighted the many facets of disparities that are still pervasive, namely income disparity, gender disparity, rural-urban disparity, and ethnic disparity.

In the context of these observations, this booklet has two major objectives. The first is to review trends of access and equity in education in the developing member countries (DMCs) of ADB. The second is to discuss trends of access and equity by country, in order to understand the various aspects and degrees of access and equity that can be related to characteristics of economic and human development.

A review as such is important because education plays an important role not only in economic development but also in the improvement of social equity. In many ways, social equity is inseparable from economic development, as improved education for all enhances the overall quality of human resources within an economy. Concerning this, ADB's *Framework and Criteria for the Appraisal and Socioeconomic Justification of Education Projects* (1994a, 5) pointed out that:

- Education can play a direct role in poverty reduction by enhancing the marketable skills of the economically disadvantaged and vulnerable groups, and by expanding their ability to take advantage of income generation possibilities and available social services.
- Education plays a key role in promoting the interests of women and increasing their diversified impact and contribution to national development goals. Women must have equal access to, and participation in, education activities.
- Through its impact on employment opportunities and earning potential, education alters the value placed on children and the willingness of parents to invest more in each child's development.
- Education contributes directly and indirectly to a higher level of socio-cultural and economic development that provides sufficient resources to address environmental issues.

The first four major sections of the booklet analyze various aspects of access and equity in DMCs over the last 20 years. The framework of analysis follows the social equity indicators set out by the above *Framework and Criteria* document (ADB 1994a, 13), namely:

- **Gender-Related Equity.** This refers to the opportunities of the traditionally disadvantaged gender group, i.e., females, in their access to various levels of education, in their opportunities for success in education, and in their opportunities to make use of education as an asset for enhancing their life chances.
- **Income-Related Equity.** This refers to the financially disadvantaged groups, i.e., the income poor, in their access to various levels of education and their opportunities for success in education.
- **Region-Related Equity.** This refers to the education opportunities of the people living in disadvantaged regions. In most cases, the disadvantaged regions are rural, but they can also be economically backward regions within an economy, and also the income poor within urban areas.
- **Sociocultural-Related Equity.** This refers to the education opportunities of socioculturally disadvantaged groups. In most cases, they are ethnic minorities within the economy, but sometimes women are also regarded as "minorities" in certain respects, and their education opportunities are limited by sociocultural perceptions of women that are unfavorable for them to receive education.

Addressing these specific aspects of equity in education coincides with a conception of education and human rights. Article 3 of the 1990 World Declaration on Education for All pointed out that:

- Basic education should be provided to all children, youth, and adults. To this end, basic education services of quality should be expanded and consistent measures must be taken to reduce disparities.
- For basic education to be equitable, all children, youth and adults must be given the opportunity to achieve and maintain an acceptable level of learning.
- The most urgent priority is to ensure access to, and improve the quality of, education for girls and women, and to remove every obstacle that hampers their active participation. All gender stereotyping in education should be eliminated.
- An active commitment must be made to remove education disparities. Underserved groups, such as the poor; street and working children; rural and remote populations; nomads and migrant workers; indigenous peoples; ethnic, racial, and linguistic minorities; refugees; those displaced by war; and people under occupation, should not suffer any discrimination in access to learning opportunities.

The agenda of the World Declaration on Education for All is by nature a concern for access and equity, covering the gender aspect and the underserved groups (or disadvantaged groups in this context). In addition, current conceptions of human rights include a variety of aspects, such as economic rights, social rights, and cultural rights; all these aspects are related to equal access to education provision for all. The framework for analysis in the booklet is therefore tuned to these various aspects of equity and rights in relation to education.

Following this analysis, the booklet explores patterns of access and equity by country groupings. DMCs are categorized into three major groups, mainly based on the Human Development Index (HDI) and the Gender-related Development Index (GDI) accorded to them by UNDP, as published in the *Human Development Reports*. The first group (Group L) consists of South Asian countries having low HDI, low GDI, and low GNP per capita. The second group (Group M) consists mainly of countries having medium HDI, medium GDI, and medium GNP per capita. However, there are some variations in this group in terms of regional locations and income. More than half of them are located in Southeast Asia and the Pacific, and two thirds of them have medium GNP per capita; but the others are scattered regionally and fall into the low GNP per capita category. The third group (Group H) consists of the four NIEs, having high HDI, high GDI, and high GNP per capita.

These indicators are adopted in order to permit understanding of the threefold relationship between economic development, human development, and education opportunities. In general, the HPAEs are located in East Asia, and the obviously low-performing economies are located mainly in South Asia. However, the less distinctive high-performing or low-performing economies, and those in the middle range, are more difficult to distinguish.

Gender-Related Equity

Despite stated recognition of females' economic and political contributions in official documents and even in laws, in general the improvement of gender-related equity remains lip service in Asia. The UNDP *Human Development Report 1997* observes that "no society treats its women as well as its men." Gender disparity is a persistent social issue that is difficult to resolve, despite general improvements in economic and social conditions. The *Human Development Reports* underscore the shortfall of opportunities for women in the areas of economic and political participation. The reports elaborate as follows:

(i)   *No society treats its women as well as its men.* This is obvious from the GDI values. A value of 1 would indicate maximum achievement in basic capabilities with perfect gender equality. However, no society achieves such a value. As many as 29 countries in the *Human Development Report 1999* have GDI values below 0.500, showing that women suffer the double deprivation of gender disparity and low achievement. Only 40 countries in this *Report* have GDI values above 0.800, showing that substantial progress in gender equality has been made in only a few societies.

(ii) *Gender inequality is strongly associated with human poverty.* The three countries ranking lowest in the GDI – Burkina Faso, Ethiopia, and Niger – also rank lowest in the HDI. From a different perspective, of the three developing countries ranking highest in the Human Poverty Index (HPI), two – Barbados and Uruguay – also rank among the highest in the GDI.

(iii) *Gender equity is not necessarily associated with high economic growth.* During the 1980s and 1990s, Botswana and Thailand enjoyed high per capita income growth and also maintained GDI ranks higher than their HDI ranks. But the Republic of Korea and the Syrian Arab Republic, despite good growth rates, had GDI ranks lower than their HDI ranks.

(iv) *The countries showing a marked improvement in their GDI ranks relative to their HDI ranks are fairly diverse.* They include industrialized countries, such as Australia and Sweden; Eastern European and Commonwealth of Independent States (CIS) countries, such as the Czech Republic and Slovenia; and less developed countries, such as Thailand and Uruguay. Thus, gender equality can be achieved across income levels, political ideologies, cultures, and stages of development (UNDP 1996, 32-3; 1997, 39; 1998, 32, 131-3; 1999, 28, 138-41).

Table 1 shows that most DMCs have GDI rankings higher than HDI rankings (in the sense that the higher the ranking, the better the status of gender and human development compared with other countries in the world).

Table 1: GDI and HDI Ranking in DMCs, 1997

Economy	HDI Rank[a]	GDI Rank	GEM Rank	GDI Value	GEM Value	HDI Rank minus GDI Rank
Singapore	22	22	32	0.83	0.51	0
Hong Kong, China	24	24	—	0.88	—	0
Korea, Republic of	30	30	78	0.85	0.34	(1)
Malaysia	56	52	52	0.76	0.45	(1)
Fiji Islands	61	60	79	0.75	0.33	(4)
Thailand	67	58	64	0.75	0.41	2
Samoa	70	—	—	—	—	—
Kazakhstan	76	64	—	0.74	—	3
Philippines	77	65	45	0.74	0.48	3
Sri Lanka	90	76	80	0.71	0.32	2
Uzbekistan	92	—	—	—	—	—
Maldives	93	77	76	0.71	0.34	2
Kyrgyz Republic	97	—	—	—	—	—
People's Republic of China	98	79	40	0.70	0.49	2
Indonesia	105	88	71	0.68	0.36	0
Tajikistan	108	92	—	0.66	—	(1)
Viet Nam	110	91	—	0.66	—	2
Vanuatu	116	—	—	—	—	—
Solomon Islands	118	—	—	—	—	—
Mongolia	119	99	—	0.62	—	1
Myanmar	128	104	—	0.58	—	2
Papua New Guinea	129	107	91	0.56	0.26	0
India	132	112	95	0.53	0.24	(3)
Cambodia	137	—	—	—	—	—
Pakistan	138	116	101	0.47	0.18	(2)
Lao People's Democratic Republic	140	115	—	0.48	—	—
Nepal	144	121	—	0.44	—	(2)
Bhutan	145	119	—	0.44	—	1
Bangladesh	150	123	83	0.43	0.30	1
Economy with the highest HDI: *Canada*	1	1	4	0.93	0.94	0
Economy with the lowest HDI: *Sierra Leone*	174	—	—	—	0.27	—
All developing countries	—	—	—	0.63	—	—
Least developed countries	—	—	—	0.42	—	—
Industrialized countries	—	—	—	0.92	—	—
World	—	—	—	0.70	—	—

— Data not available.
GDI = Gender-related Development Index.
GEM = Gender Empowerment Measure.
HDI = Human Development Index.
Note: Data in parentheses are negative.
[a] Table is sorted by this column heading.

Source: UNDP 1999, 138-45.

This seems to suggest that DMCs have paid substantial attention to gender development alongside broader human development. However, the favorable GDI rankings of DMCs, compared with the HDI rankings, should be balanced by the following considerations:

- DMCs' GDIs are generally low compared with countries outside Asia,

especially the members of the Organisation for Economic Co-operation and Development (OECD).

- The HPAEs, plus Fiji Islands, although ranked top in HDI among
  DMCs, all have Gender Empowerment Measure (GEM) rankings lower
  than their HDI ranks. For example, Singapore's HDI and GEM ranks
  were 22 and 32, and the Republic of Korea's ranks were 30 and 78.
- Among the 174 countries presented in the *Human Development
  Report 1999*, only 12 of the 29 DMCs' GDIs were in the upper-middle
  ranks, i.e., above the value of 0.700.
- Although their GEM ranks were not as low as their GDI ranks, as
  compared with a total of 102 countries being ranked, all GEM values
  were significantly lower than the GDI values.

These facts mean that most DMCs still rank low in gender development
compared with other parts of the world.

It is not difficult to find a parallel phenomenon in education. A review of
education attainments in the last two or three decades in DMCs suggests that
there are overall improvements in literacy and school enrollments, but that
females remain a disadvantaged group compared with males.

Literacy

According to figures from the United Nations Educational, Scientific and
Cultural Organization (UNESCO), despite a general improvement in literacy in
Asia, the illiterate adult population grew from 638 million in 1970 to 700 million
in 1990. This was because improvements in education provision could not
keep abreast with increases in population.

The growth in the size of the illiterate population was partly attributable to
the increase of female illiterates from 392 million to 446 million during the
period. Such an increase outweighed the effect of a decrease in male illiterates

**Table 2: Estimated Change of Out-of-School Children by Gender in South
Asia, 1990-1995**

Country	Female 1995 (%)[a]	Change total ('000)	Male ('000)	Female ('000)	Female/ Male
Iran	93.8	-115	4	-119	29.8
India	75.1	4,854	1,912	2,942	1.5
Nepal	66.4	212	211	1	0
Maldives	57.1	-1	-1	0	0
Pakistan	55.7	1,358	394	964	2.5
Bangladesh	55.3	319	137	182	1.3
Afghanistan	52.5	596	279	317	1.1
Bhutan	50.2	23	15	8	0.5
Sri Lanka	25.0	-3	-2	-1	0.5
South Asia	65.9	7,127	2,885	4,242	1.5

[a] Table is sorted by this column heading.

Source: UNESCO-PROAP 1996, 19.

Table 3: Adult Literacy Rates by Gender in DMCs, 1985 and 1998

Economy	1985[a]			1998[b]		
	Male (%)	Female (%)	Male/ Female	Male (%)	Female (%)	Male/ Female[c]
Afghanistan	37	8	4.6	47	15	3.1
Nepal	32	9	3.6	41	14	2.9
Pakistan	35	15	2.3	50	24	2.1
Bhutan	46	19	2.4	56	28	2.0
Bangladesh	40	18	2.2	49	26	1.9
India	55	26	2.1	66	38	1.7
Lao PDR	92	76	1.2	69	44	1.6
Cambodia	—	—	—	80	53	1.5
Papua New Guinea	74	52	1.4	81	63	1.3
China, People's Republic of	79	51	1.5	90	73	1.2
Indonesia	78	58	1.3	90	78	1.2
Singapore	93	78	1.2	90	73	1.2
Hong Kong, China	95	82	1.2	96	88	1.1
Malaysia	80	60	1.3	89	78	1.1
Myanmar	86	72	1.2	89	78	1.1
Sri Lanka	91	82	1.1	93	87	1.1
Viet Nam	93	83	1.1	97	91	1.1
Fiji Islands	90	84	1.1	94	89	1.1
Taipei, China	96	85	1.1	98	91	1.1
Thailand	93	85	1.1	96	92	1.0
Korea, Republic of	98	93	1.1	99	97	1.0
Kyrgyz Republic	99	96	1.0	100	100	1.0
Kazakhstan	99	96	1.0	100	100	1.0
Tajikistan	99	97	1.0	100	100	1.0
Maldives	92	92	1.0	93	93	1.0
Uzbekistan	99	96	1.0	100	100	1.0
Micronesia, Fed. States of	—	—	—	95	93	1.0
Philippines	84	83	1.0	95	94	1.0
Mongolia	89	77	1.2	—	—	—

— Data not available.
Note: Data refer to population 15-45 years old.
[a] Data relate to years 1980 through 1989.
[b] Data relate to years 1990 through 1998.
[c] Table is sorted by this column heading.

Sources: ADB 1999, 256; UNESCO, Division of Statistics 1999.

by 5 million since 1980. Moreover, Asia and the Pacific has accounted for more than three quarters of adult illiterates in the developing world (UNESCO, Division of Statistics 1993, 8). In 1995, there were 167 million illiterate adults in East Asia, 38 million in Southeast Asia and the Pacific, and 407 million in South Asia (UNDP 1997, 27). In terms of proportion, according to a 1997 ADB report (p.279), adult female literacy rates rose from 17 percent to 35 percent between 1970 and 1993, while in East Asia they rose from 55 percent to 72 percent.

Literate females are still a minority in South Asia, and a large proportion of illiterates in Asia come from the South Asian subregion. In Bangladesh, India, Nepal, and Pakistan, women's illiteracy exceeded men's by 20 percentage points or more. The figures on illiteracy matched the growth of the out-of-school population. Between 1990 and 1995, the estimated number of out-of-school children grew by 7,127,000. Among these were 4,854,000 in India and

1,358,000 in Pakistan. However, the Maldives and Sri Lanka were successful in achieving a slight reduction in the out-of-school population: 1,000 in the former and 3,000 in the latter (Table 2).

Table 3 shows that several Asian countries have achieved an equal literacy ratio between males and females. These countries include four central Asian republics (Kazakhstan, Kyrgyz Republic, Tajikistan, and Uzbekistan), Republic of Korea, Maldives, Philippines, and Thailand. Many other Asian economies have been able to bring the male/female literacy ratios very close to parity. They are mostly East and Southeast Asian economies, such as People's Republic of China (PRC); Hong Kong, China; Indonesia; Lao People's Democratic Republic (Lao PDR); Malaysia; Myanmar; Singapore; Taipei, China; and Viet Nam. Gender disparity in literacy is clear in South Asia. In 1998, the male/female literacy ratio was 1.5 in Cambodia, 1.7 in India, 1.9 in Bangladesh, 2.0 in Bhutan, 2.1 in Pakistan, 2.9 in Nepal, and 3.1 in Afghanistan.

There are also obvious differences between age groups among females. Improvements in literacy are evident for the younger generation. For example, in 1980 in Singapore the female literacy rate was 96 percent for the 15-24 age group, but was only 69 percent for the 35-44 age group. In Pakistan, the literacy rate among the younger age group was only 25 percent, but at 11 percent it was even lower for the older age group (ADB 1993, 73).

In addition, there is a gap between urban and rural residents. For

Table 4: Adult Illiteracy Rates by Gender in DMCs, 1995

Economy	Female (%)	Male (%)	Female/Male[a]
Singapore	14	4	3.6
Hong Kong, China	12	4	3.0
Korea, Republic of	3	1	3.0
China, People's Republic of	27	10	2.7
Viet Nam	9	4	2.3
Indonesia	22	10	2.2
Mongolia	23	11	2.1
Malaysia	22	11	2.0
Myanmar	22	11	2.0
Thailand	8	4	2.0
Papua New Guinea	37	19	1.9
Sri Lanka	13	7	1.9
Fiji Islands	11	6	1.8
India	62	35	1.8
Lao People's Democratic Republic	56	31	1.8
Afghanistan	85	53	1.6
Bhutan	72	44	1.6
Bangladesh	74	51	1.5
Nepal	86	59	1.5
Pakistan	76	50	1.5
Philippines	6	5	1.2
Cambodia	9	9	1.0
Taipei,China	7	7	1.0
Maldives	7	7	1.0

Note: Data refer to population of people 15 years old and above.
[a] Table is sorted by this column heading.

Sources: Lewin 1996, 92; UNDP 1997, 164-5.

example, in Afghanistan, urban female literacy rates have been recorded as eight times higher than rural female literacy rates. In the Philippines, the urban female literacy rate was recorded as 97 percent, compared with 85 percent in rural areas (ADB 1993, 73). In 1991/92, over two million children in the PRC were not enrolled in school, of whom 70 percent were girls; and in many rural areas women constitute 70 percent of the illiterate population (UNDP 1997, 50).

In conclusion, although literacy has been generally improved, females obviously constitute the larger proportion of the illiterate population in Asia (Table 4).

Education Attainments

Between 1970 and 1990, girls' participation in education improved from 41.6 percent to 43.1 percent in overall enrollment, from 43.4 percent to 45.2 percent in primary enrollment, from 39.7 percent to 42.1 percent in secondary enrollment, and from 36.6 percent to 38.0 percent in tertiary enrollment. However, in terms of absolute numbers, girls' enrollment has continued to be lower than boys' (UNESCO, Division of Statistics 1993, 12, Table 8). This pattern, and the underlying factors, are here examined by level of education.

Primary Enrollments

During the period 1980 to 1990, primary education enrollments in Asia and the Pacific grew from 348 million to 373 million, representing a steady annual growth of about 0.7 percent. However, girls' enrollments grew faster than boys'. Girls' enrollments accounted for 45.2 percent of the total at the primary level in 1990, compared with 43.7 percent in 1980. Considerable progress was seen in some low-performing Asian economies. In Bangladesh, for example, enrollments grew by 76 percent during this period, raising the proportion of girls in total enrollments from 37 percent to 45 percent in 1990 (UNESCO, Division of Statistics 1993, 14).

During the 1990s, the primary gross enrollment rates (GERs) reached nearly 100 percent for both boys and girls in most DMCs located in East and Southeast Asia, including the PRC. GERs in South Asian countries were lower during the 1980s. However, even in that region by 1998 most had exceeded 70 percent and some even approached 100 percent. The chief exception was Afghanistan where enrollment rates remained at around 50 percent (Table 5).

The male/female ratio of enrollment in Asia has tended to approach parity over time. The higher-income DMCs reached parity in the mid-1980s. In Mongolia, girls' enrollment rates have even been slightly higher than boys' (1:1.1 in 1998). DMCs where boys' primary enrollment rates remain higher than girls' are Bangladesh, Cambodia, India, Lao PDR, Nepal, Papua New Guinea, and Solomon Islands, ranging from 1.2:1 to 1.5:1. However, as shown in Table 5, the boy/girl enrollment ratios in Afghanistan (2:1) and Pakistan (2.2:1) remain notably high.

Equity and Access to Education

Table 5: Primary GERs by Gender in DMCs, 1985 and 1998

Economy	1985[a]				1998[b]			
	Total (%)	Male (%)	Female (%)	Male/ Female	Total (%)	Male (%)	Female (%)	Male/ Female[c]
East Asia								
Hong Kong, China	106	106	105	1.0	96	99	99	1.0
Korea, Republic of	97	100	100	1.0	101	98	99	1.0
PRC	123	132	114	1.2	118	120	116	1.0
Taipei,China	—	99	100	1.0	—	100	102	1.0
Mongolia	103	107	107	1.0	88	82	87	0.9
Central Asia								
Kazakhstan	88	88	87	1.0	96	86	86	1.0
Kyrgyz Republic	122	123	123	1.0	107	110	111	1.0
Tajikistan	85	86	85	1.0	91	91	88	1.0
Uzbekistan	87	88	85	1.0	77	78	76	1.0
South Asia								
Pakistan	44	56	30	1.9	74	94	42	2.2
Afghanistan	20	27	13	2.1	49	63	32	2.0
Nepal	80	101	47	2.1	110	130	87	1.5
Bangladesh	63	72	54	1.3	78	84	73	1.2
India	96	111	79	1.4	100	115	93	1.2
Maldives	141	156	148	1.0	134	136	133	1.0
Sri Lanka	103	104	101	1.0	113	106	104	1.0
Southeast Asia and Pacific								
Lao PDR	111	121	100	1.2	107	123	92	1.3
Cambodia	248	209	174	1.2	122	130	106	1.2
Papua New Guinea	63	66	51	1.3	00	88	75	1.2
Solomon Islands	00	85	65	1.3	97	104	90	1.2
Viet Nam	103	106	100	1.1	114	118	112	1.1
Fiji Islands	122	122	122	1.0	128	128	127	1.0
Indonesia	117	120	114	1.1	114	117	113	1.0
Malaysia	101	101	100	1.0	91	93	93	1.0
Micronesia, Fed. States of	—	—	—	—	—	94	94	1.0
Myanmar	98	101	96	1.1	103	112	108	1.0
Philippines	107	108	107	1.0	116	117	116	1.0
Samoa	—	87	90	1.0	116	106	107	1.0
Singapore	111	120	114	1.1	95	99	98	1.0
Thailand	96	100	97	1.0	87	98	97	1.0
Vanuatu	100	103	98	1.1	106	105	107	1.0

— Data not available.
GER = gross enrollment rate.
[a] Data are for 1980-89.
[b] Data are for 1990-98.
[c] Table is sorted in subregional groups by this column heading.

Sources: ADB 1999, 256; UNDP 1998, 162-3; UNESCO, Division of Statistics 1999.

Secondary Enrollments

Enrollments in secondary education in Asia and the Pacific increased from 155 million in 1980 to 191 million in 1990, at an average annual growth rate of 2.1 percent. Compared with the 5 percent growth rate in the 1970s, the rate of growth in the 1980s was much slower (UNESCO, Division of Statistics 1993, 20). While primary GERs in most DMCs approached 100 percent in the 1990s, GERs at the secondary level in about half the DMCs were below 50 percent. In South Asia, secondary schools served only about one third of the relevant age group (Table 6).

Table 6: Secondary GERs by Gender in DMCs, 1985 and 1998

Economy	1985[a]				1998[b]			
	Total (%)	Male (%)	Female (%)	Male/ Female	Total (%)	Male (%)	Female (%)	Male/ Female[c]
East Asia								
PRC	40	45	33	1.4	67	60	51	1.2
Korea, Rep. of	92	92	88	1.0	101	98	98	1.0
Taipei,China	—	89	91	1.0	—	96	99	1.0
Hong Kong, China	71	69	73	0.9	75	73	78	0.9
Mongolia	91	85	97	0.9	59	50	70	0.7
Central Asia								
Tajikistan	113	113	113	1.0	79	83	75	1.1
Uzbekistan	107	117	97	1.2	93	99	87	1.1
Kazakhstan	103	102	104	1.0	83	89	92	1.0
Kyrgyz Republic	109	111	108	1.0	81	84	89	0.9
South Asia								
Afghanistan	8	11	5	2.2	22	32	11	2.9
Nepal	25	37	12	3.1	51	46	23	2.0
Bangladesh	18	26	11	2.4	19	25	13	1.9
Pakistan	17	24	10	2.4	30	33	17	1.9
India	38	62	35	1.8	49	80	55	1.5
Maldives	21	21	22	1.0	49	49	49	1.0
Sri Lanka	63	60	60	1.0	75	71	79	0.9
Southeast Asia and Pacific								
Cambodia	29	36	21	1.7	27	31	18	1.7
Lao PDR	24	27	19	1.4	25	31	19	1.6
Papua New Guinea	12	15	8	1.9	14	17	11	1.5
Solomon Islands	19	22	9	2.4	17	21	14	1.5
Indonesia	41	50	41	1.2	48	49	41	1.2
Vanuatu	15	18	14	1.3	20	23	19	1.2
Fiji Islands	51	51	51	1.0	64	64	65	1.0
Myanmar	23	24	22	1.1	30	23	23	1.0
Singapore	62	89	95	0.9	73	72	74	1.0
Thailand	30	30	28	1.1	55	38	37	1.0
Malaysia	53	53	53	1.0	57	58	64	0.9
Micronesia, Fed. States of	—	—	—	—	—	78	85	0.9
Philippines	64	64	65	1.0	79	78	83	0.9
Samoa	67	61	67	0.9	47	67	71	0.9
Viet Nam	43	44	41	1.1	47	—	—	—

— Data not available.
[a] Data relate to years 1980 through 1989.
[b] Data relate to years 1990 through 1998.
[c] Table is sorted in subregional groups by this column heading.

Sources: ADB 1999, 256; UNDP 1998, 162-3; UNESCO, Division of Statistics 1999.

While enrollment is approaching gender parity at the primary level, at the secondary level the disparity widens. Table 6 suggests that in only a few DMCs are male/female enrollment ratios 1:1. These DMCs are Taipei, China; Fiji Islands; Kazakhstan; Republic of Korea; Maldives; Myanmar; Singapore; and Thailand. In many countries, the male/female enrollment ratios are slightly higher on the male side (1.1:1 to 1.7:1), including Cambodia, PRC, India, Indonesia, Lao PDR, Papua New Guinea, Solomon Islands, Tajikistan, Uzbekistan, and Vanuatu. DMCs with significantly higher male enrollment rates (1.9:1 and above) are Afghanistan, Bangladesh, Nepal, and Pakistan. It is interesting to note that there are also some DMCs where the male enrollment rates are slightly lower than the female rates. These DMCs are Hong Kong, China; Kyrgyz Republic; Malaysia; Mongolia; Federated States of Micronesia; Philippines; Samoa; and Sri Lanka.

The gender gap is even more obvious in the completion rates. In Indonesia and Marshall Islands, the completion rate for boys has been two or three times as high as that for girls. However, in a few Asian countries the completion rates are close to equal or more favorable on the boys' side (about 1.4:1). These are Fiji Islands, Republic of Korea, Mongolia, and Viet Nam. Across time, a clear trend of improvement can be seen. For example, the male/female completion rate dropped from 4.1 in 1970 to 3.1 in 1980 in India; and between 1980 and 1990, from 3 to 1 in Maldives, and from 2.5 to 1.4 in Fiji Islands. However, in 1980, the male/female rate was as high as 9.9 in Afghanistan, 6.1 in Bangladesh, and 5.6 in Nepal (see Appendix 1, Table A1.1).

Tertiary Enrollments

Total enrollment in higher education in Asia and the Pacific grew from 11 million in 1970 to 26 million in 1990, more than doubling within two decades. However, female participation in higher education improved only slightly from 36.6 percent in 1970 to 38.0 percent in 1990 (UNESCO, Division of Statistics 1993, 25, 27). While many DMCs could only reach a male/female ratio of below 2:1 at the secondary level, in most of them the ratio was 3:1 at the tertiary level.

The largest gap was found in Bangladesh and Nepal, with respective male/female ratios of 7.3:1 and 5.0:1 around 1980 (Table 7). In the major universities in Cambodia, females accounted for only 12 to 15 percent of the student population, and their representation was as low as 1.5 percent and 4.6 percent in the technological institutes and the Royal University of Agriculture in 1993/94 (ADB 1996c, 18). The 15 percent of female representation in tertiary institutions was much lower than the 45 percent in primary schools, 40 percent in lower secondary schools, and 25 percent in upper secondary schools (UNDP 1996, 40).

In general, the higher the education level, the lower the female representation. For example, in Indonesia the percentage of female students declined from 48 percent in primary enrollments to 32 percent in tertiary enrollments (1994), from 47 percent to 30 percent in Viet Nam (1994), and from 45 percent to 16 percent in Bangladesh (1990). This pattern has remained unchanged for a long period, although the percentage of females did rise from 22 percent in 1970 to 38 percent in 1994 in Indonesia, and from 14 percent in 1980 to 16 percent in 1990 in Bangladesh (ADB 1996e, 9; Chowdhury 1997, 6; Indonesia, Ministry of Education and Culture 1997, 74). Statistics also indicate some gender stereotyping in the fields of study. Males and females tend to cluster in different fields of study, which has implications for their occupational opportunities. In Kiribati, for example, females account for 100 percent of enrollments in home economics, 85 percent in library studies, and over 50 percent in such social science subjects as education, geography, history/politics, and sociology. Subjects that may lead to high incomes (such as economics and technology) are dominated by males, who make up over 90 percent of the enrollments. Moreover, male students have better shares in overseas scholarships for higher education or training (Emberson-Bain 1995, 22). In Cambodia, females account for less than 1 percent of the enrollments in such tertiary courses as architecture, electricity, hydrology, law and economics, but have a higher proportion of enrollments in commerce (16 percent), teacher training (23 percent), and foreign languages (23 percent) (ADB 1996c, 19). Professional courses are also dominated by males in Hong Kong, China. At the University of Hong Kong, male/female enrollment rates in the early 1990s were 32:1 in engineering, 4.3:1 in medicine, and 4.7:1 in dentistry (Westwood, Mehrain, and Cheung 1995, 39).

Table 7: Population of University Graduates by Gender in DMCs, 1970s-1990s

Economy	Circa 1970			Circa 1980			Latest		
	M%	F%	M/F	M%	F%	M/F[a]	M%	F%	M/F
Bangladesh	—	—	—	2.2	0.3	7.3	—	—	—
Nepal	—	—	—	1.0	0.2	5.0	—	—	—
Afghanistan	1.7	0.3	5.7	12.5	2.7	4.6	—	—	—
Pakistan	—	—	—	2.7	0.7	3.9	—	—	—
India	1.7	0.3	5.7	3.2	0.9	3.6	—	—	—
Korea, Republic of	6.5	1.1	5.9	10.5	2.8	3.4	12.2	3.9	3.1
Malaysia	—	—	—	1.7	0.5	3.4	—	—	—
Tonga	—	—	—	0.9	0.3	3.0	—	—	—
Taipei,China	—	—	—	6.8	2.5	2.7	—	—	—
PRC	—	—	—	1.3	0.5	2.6	—	—	—
Marshall Islands	—	—	—	—	—	—	15.7	6.8	2.3
Hong Kong, China	6.5	2.5	2.6	7.1	3.2	2.2	—	—	—
Viet Nam	—	—	—	—	—	—	3.7	1.7	2.2
Singapore	—	—	—	17.0	8.4	2.0	—	—	—
Indonesia	0.8	0.1	8.0	1.7	0.8	2.1	1.9	0.6	3.2
Vanuatu	—	—	—	4.3	2.5	1.7	—	—	—
Fiji Islands	—	—	—	4.1	2.5	1.6	5.3	3.4	1.2
Sri Lanka	1.0	0.4	2.5	2.2	1.5	1.5	—	—	—
Myanmar	—	—	—	1.4	1.2	1.2	—	—	—
Thailand	1.2	0.5	2.4	2.7	2.2	1.2	—	—	—
Maldives	—	—	—	0.1	0.0	1.0	0.3	0.1	3.0
Philippines	10.4	8.8	1.2	9.2	10.5	0.9	—	—	—

— Data not available.
[a] Table is sorted by this column heading.

Source: ADB 1993, 158-60.

Gender imbalances in enrollment are also wide in vocational education programs. In Viet Nam, females are concentrated in Teachers' Colleges, Nursing Schools, and Schools of Social Work, and in courses such as library science, accounting, and secretarial work, i.e., in courses associated with the nurturing and service-sector roles that society ascribes to women. They are enrolled in only one of the three agricultural schools and the admission is limited to 20 percent of places, a situation that appears to reflect the 'invisibility' of women in the official agricultural labor force. In the 28 technical colleges, only about 30 percent of the students are women. However, they constitute 75 to 80 percent of the students in commercial courses, while the percentage receiving technical education has been minimal (McDonald 1995, 5).

Dropout and Repetition

GER, as an indication of total enrollment in education expressed as a percentage of population of relevant age group, can only represent a partial picture of access to education. This is because a high GER can be a result of significant numbers of overage enrollment and repetition. UNESCO's *Mid-decade Review* (UNESCO-Principal Regional Office for Asia and the Pacific [PROAP] 1996, 25) pointed out that "increasingly, the principal quantitative problem in the subregion is no longer that of simply enrolling children, but that of ensuring their retention and progress through their grades."

When looking at repetition and retention rates, the picture of access in education can be very different. Tables 8 and 9 show that the access rates to Primary Grade I are quite high across DMCs. However, the retention rates are distinctively low in South Asia. In 1992, only 32 and 39 percent of Primary Grade 1 students survived to Grade 5 in Bhutan and Pakistan respectively; and 50 and 56 percent respectively in Bangladesh and the Lao PDR. UNESCO

Table 8: Access and Retention in Primary Education in Selected DMCs, 1992

| Country | Apparent access rate to Primary Grade 1 (%) | Grade 1 students get to primary | | Population get to Grade 5 (%)[a] | Primary internal efficiency ratio |
		Grade 2 (%)	Grade 5 (%)		
Bhutan	66	93	49	32	0.6
Pakistan	74	81	51	39	0.7
Bangladesh	101	77	52	50	0.7
China, People's Republic of	104	98	88	91	0.9
Lao PDR	118	74	47	56	0.5
Nepal	125	66	52	65	0.6
India	133	97	62	82	0.7
Sri Lanka	95	98	92	87	0.9
Philippines	136	87	65	88	0.8
Indonesia	110	98	86	94	0.8
All	106	87	63	68	0.7

[a] Table is sorted by this column heading.

Source: Chuard and Mingat 1996b, 3.

Table 9: Repetition and Retention Rates in DMCs, 1980s and 1990s
(percent)

Economy	Repeaters Total 1985	1995	Male 1985	1995	Female 1985	1995	1994 Cohort Reaching Grade 2 M	F	Total	Grade 3 M	F	Total
Afghanistan	6	9	6	9	6	9	—	—	—	—	—	—
Cambodia	—	30	—	31	—	30	84	81	83	56	42	50
PRC	7	2	—	2	—	2	99	99	99	92	92	92
Hong Kong, China	2	1	2	—	2	—	—	—	—	—	—	100
India	4	—	4	—	4	—	81	81	81	65	69	62
Indonesia	11	8	—	8	—	7	100	94	97	96	81	90
Kazakhstan	—	0	—	0	—	0	—	—	—	—	—	—
Kyrgyz Republic	—	0	—	—	—	—	—	—	—	—	—	92
Lao PDR	27	26	—	27	—	25	74	72	73	55	51	53
Malaysia	—	—	—	—	—	—	95	95	95	94	94	94
Maldives	—	—	—	—	—	—	94	96	95	91	94	93
Mongolia	—	1	—	1	—	0	95	96	96	—	—	—
Nepal	21	27	—	28	—	24	68	62	65	52	52	52
Philippines	2	—	2	—	2	—	—	—	84	—	—	70
Korea, Republic of	—	—	—	—	—	—	100	100	100	100	100	100
Singapore	1	—	1	—	1	—	—	—	—	—	—	—
Sri Lanka	8	—	8	—	9	—	100	100	100	98	98	98

— Data not available.

Source: UNESCO, Division of Statistics 1999.

figures also show that the percentages of the 1994 cohort able to survive to Grade 3 were quite close to the 1992 figures for Grade 5, i.e., about 50 percent in Cambodia, India, and Lao PDR. In Nepal, dropout rates have increased rather than decreased (Thapa 1996, 2). Repetition rates are in general below 10 percent in DMCs, but again are relatively high in South Asia. They are about one quarter in Nepal and Lao PDR, and one third in Cambodia (UNESCO, Division of Statistics 1999).

Table 9 shows that, except in Cambodia (where girls' retention rate was obviously low: 42 percent compared with boys' 56 percent), there are no distinctive gender differences in retention rates across DMCs. In some cases, girls' retention rates can even be higher than boys': for example, 69 percent versus 65 percent in India. However, this does not necessarily mean that girls have better access to education. On the contrary, this may only mean that the girls who can enter schools (probably those who are from better-off families) have a higher tendency to push through with their education. Chuard and Mingat (1996b, 3) note particularly that the relatively low coverage of primary education in South Asia concerns both boys and girls, but gender differences are on average stronger in South Asia than elsewhere in the region. The ratio between the GERs of girls and boys was estimated at 0.69, against 0.89 in other sampled countries.

Many factors can lead to dropouts. A Nepalese report (Thapa 1996) has identified a number of school-related and family-related factors that may apply to many other contexts. As shown in Table 10, school-related factors include unfavorable school facilities, low quality of teachers, medium of

Table 10: Causes of Dropout and Repetition

School-related factors	Family-related factors
1. Lack of adequate physical facilities: • crowded classrooms • inclusion of primary grades in secondary schools	1. Poor economic conditions: • inability to purchase stationery • inability to purchase school dress • inability to provide additional financial support to school-going children
2. Teachers' performance: • low quality of teaching • teacher absenteeism • poor behavior with students	2. Children have to work: • looking after younger siblings • doing household chores • working at farm
3. Language problem: • the medium of instruction in school is not a spoken language to many or most children	3. Lack of awareness of the importance of education • low level of parental education • parents being indifferent to children • irregularity in school attendance
4. Student's low learning outcomes.	4. Gender discrimination: • girls taken out of school after reaching certain grades
5. Lack of effective need-based scholarship and studentships.	5. Sending underage children to school, but lack of preschool facilities.

Source: Adapted from Thapa 1996, 1, Table 20.

instruction, low student performance, and unavailability of studentships. Family-related factors include the requirement for children to work, a lack of awareness of the significance of education, gender discrimination, and insufficient child-care facilities.

Life Chances Beyond Education

Despite a general improvement in education opportunities for females, their participation rate in the labor force has remained more or less constant over the last 20 years. In most DMCs, women's shares of the adult labor force range between 35 and 45 percent. The greatest increases in female participation in the labor force has taken place in Fiji Islands and Sri Lanka, where the rates grew from 12 and 25 percent in 1970 to 23 and 34 percent in 1990, respectively (Table 11).

In Indonesia and Sri Lanka, the unemployment rates of women are higher than those of men across all levels of education. The Indonesian figures show that the higher their level of education, the higher their rate of unemployment. The highest rates of unemployment are among those with general upper secondary education and university education. It seems that people taking a vocational stream of secondary education stand a better chance of employment. Although this phenomenon applies to both genders, the educated females are more vulnerable to unemployment, as their unemployment rates at the diploma and university levels are over twice those of males. Such a gender differentiation also occurs among those with vocational lower secondary education. However, males with vocational lower secondary education have very low rates of unemployment, while females' rates remain high (Table 12). A similar situation exists in Sri Lanka, i.e., the higher the level of education, the

Table 11: Women's Share of Adult Labor Force in DMCs, 1970 and 1995 (percent)

Economy	1970	1995[a]	Economy	1970	1995[a]
Cambodia	49	52	Bhutan	40	39
Viet Nam	48	50	Indonesia	30	39
Lao PDR	45	47	Korea, Republic of	32	39
Thailand	48	47	Singapore	26	38
Mongolia	46	46	Hong Kong, China	35	37
PRC	42	45	Philippines	33	37
Myanmar	44	44	Malaysia	31	36
Bangladesh	40	42	Sri Lanka	25	34
Maldives	38	42	India	34	31
Papua New Guinea	42	41	Pakistan	22	24
Nepal	39	40	Fiji Islands	12	23

Note: Data refer to population 15 years old and above.
[a] Table is sorted by this column heading.

Source: UNDP 1998, 164-5.

Table 12: Unemployment by Level of Education and Gender in Indonesia, 1994

School level	Female (%)	Male (%)	Female/Male
No schooling	0.4	0.4	1.0
Incomplete primary	1.1	0.8	1.4
Complete primary	3.2	2.0	1.6
Junior high school (General)	8.2	5.5	1.5
Junior high school (Vocational)	10.5	4.5	2.3
Senior high school (General)	24.9	13.6	1.8
Senior high school (Vocational)	14.8	8.9	1.7
Diploma	14.9	7.2	2.1
University	24.9	10.3	2.4
Total	5.1	3.9	1.3

Source : World Bank 1996b, 68.

Table 13: Unemployment by Level of Education and Gender in Sri Lanka, 1980s

Level of education	1981/82			1985/86		
	M%	F%	F/M	M%	F%	F/M
No schooling (Illiterate)	2.6	2.1	1.2	4.8	7.7	0.6
No schooling (Literate)	—	2.4	—	—	—	—
Primary	7.8	3.8	2.1	9.4	7.0	1.3
Secondary	33.5	9.6	3.5	25.2	12.5	2.0
GCE (Ordinary level)	42.0	14.5	2.9	35.6	14.4	2.5
GCE (Advanced level)	52.2	22.0	2.4	44.9	18.7	2.4
Undergraduates	40.0	42.9	0.9	—	—	—
Graduates and Postgraduates	12.1	8.1	1.5	6.7	3.8	1.8
Total	21.3	7.8	2.7	20.8	10.8	1.9

— Data not available.
GCE = General Certificate of Education.

Source: Jayaweera 1991, 6.

Table 14: Labor Force in Managerial and Professional Occupations by Gender in DMCs, 1970s-1990s

Economy	Circa 1970			Circa 1980			Latest		
	M%	F%	M/F	M%	F%	M/F	M%	F%	M/F
Afghanistan	—	—	—	2.9	5.4	0.5	—	—	—
Bangladesh	2.2	3.8	0.6	—	—	—	4.2	3.7	1.1
PRC	—	—	—	7.9	4.8	1.6	8.2	5.8	1.4
Cook Islands	—	—	—	17.4	23.6	0.7	—	—	—
Fiji Islands	—	—	—	7.4	20.0	0.4	7.0	14.4	0.5
Hong Kong, China	10.8	8.8	1.2	9.3	7.4	1.3	—	—	—
India	—	—	—	4.4	3.4	1.3	—	—	—
Indonesia	3.1	2.6	1.2	2.9	3.3	0.9	3.4	3.9	0.9
Kiribati	—	—	—	21.2	39.2	0.5	27.1	40.7	0.7
Korea, Republic of	5.3	2.2	2.4	6.9	3.5	2.0	9.2	7.0	1.3
Malaysia	5.6	5.3	1.1	—	—	—	—	—	—
Maldives	5.1	3.0	1.7	—	—	—	13.3	10.0	1.3
Marshall Islands	—	—	—	23.4	18.7	1.3	19.0	20.3	0.9
Myanmar	—	—	—	2.9	3.1	0.9	—	—	—
Nepal	0.8	0.2	4.0	1.5	0.5	3.0	—	—	—
Pakistan	—	—	—	4.9	17.9	0.3	—	—	—
Philippines	4.7	10.7	0.4	3.7	11.5	0.3	—	—	—
Samoa	6.4	27.3	0.2	8.4	37.5	0.2	—	—	—
Singapore	—	—	—	15.7	12.4	1.3	28.6	20.6	1.4
Solomon Islands	—	—	—	—	—	—	16.1	15.7	1.0
Sri Lanka	—	—	—	5.6	15.0	0.4	—	—	—
Taipei,China	5.7	6.6	0.9	8.2	8.9	0.9	—	—	—
Thailand	4.5	1.7	2.6	6.3	3.6	1.8	—	—	—
Tonga	—	—	—	11.4	48.3	0.2	8.6	26.1	0.3
Vanuatu	—	—	—	6.6	8.2	0.8	—	—	—
Viet Nam	—	—	—	7.0	4.9	1.4	—	—	—

— Data not available.
Note: Data refer to population 25 years old and above.

Source: ADB 1993, 191-3.

higher the rate of unemployment, and females' unemployment rates exceed males' across all levels of education. Also, females' unemployment rates among those with secondary education, General Certificate of Education (GCE) and degrees are over twice those of males (Table 13).

Looking at access to managerial and professional occupations, the situation varies across DMCs. Some countries have more males than females in these occupations, such as PRC, Republic of Korea, Maldives, and Singapore. However, the difference is not big, as in general the male/female ratio is about 1.3:1. Moreover, a number of DMCs have more females than males in these positions, for example Fiji Islands, Indonesia, Kiribati, Marshall Islands, and Tonga (Table 14). However, this does not necessarily mean that women are enjoying higher social status. For example, in Pakistan, while 18 percent of women and 5 percent of men are classified as professional and managerial, the majority of women (65 percent) but a minority of men (20 percent) are teachers (ADB 1993, 105).

Gender disparity in life chances is clearer if administrative and managerial positions are separated from other occupations. UNDP figures (1998, 154-5,

188) show that female representation is the weakest in administrative and managerial occupations, compared with the other three categories, namely, professional and technical, sales and service workers, and clerical workers. The highest representation of women in administrative and managerial occupations is found in the Philippines, where they hold about one third of the positions. The lowest representation is in India, Republic of Korea, Pakistan and Solomon Islands, where the figure is only 2 to 4 percent.

Women hold 30 to 40 percent of professional and technical positions in most DMCs, with a few at or below 20 percent (Pakistan and Sri Lanka). Sri Lanka has the lowest representation rate (19 percent), and the Philippines the highest (64 percent). Female representation in the other two types of occupations are higher than in the professional and technical occupations. In most DMCs, average female representation moves up to 40 to 50 percent for sales and services occupations, and further up to 50 to 60 percent for clerical occupations. Thus despite an improvement in access and equity for the females in education, their life chances are more open at the lower end rather than the upper end of the occupation hierarchy, except in a few DMCs where females' enrollments at all levels are comparable to or even slightly higher than those of males (see Appendix 1, Table A1.2).

In Mongolia, where females' literacy and enrollment rates are comparable to males', the occupations in which females outnumber males are nursing, sewing, food/restaurant-related work, civil service, doctors, and teaching at all levels (including professorships). However, men outnumber women in "specialist" professions, such as engineers, economists, lawyers, veterinary surgeons, and agronomists. The picture is very mixed in Mongolia, but a gender division of labor seems to be easily identified in that females mainly work as teachers whereas males work as specialists (Table 15).

Table 15: Female and Male Representation in Occupations in Mongolia, 1990

Occupation	Male (%)	Female (%)	Male/Female
People with higher education	57.5	42.5	1.4
Engineers	76.4	23.6	3.2
Veterinary surgeons	74.6	25.4	2.9
Lawyers	73.4	26.6	2.8
Livestock specialists	70.5	29.5	2.4
Economists	58.1	41.9	1.4
Computer and electronic technology engineers	57.6	42.4	1.4
Agronomists	55.4	44.6	1.2
Teachers and Professors	44.8	55.2	0.8
Doctors	31.7	68.3	0.5
Public servants	25.9	74.1	0.3
People with vocational training	38.3	61.7	0.6
Technicians/Operators	61.4	38.6	1.6
Elementary schoolteachers	26.2	73.8	0.4
Food industry	21.2	78.8	0.3
Nurses	16.9	83.1	0.2
Sewing	11.4	88.6	0.1
Restaurant cooks	12.2	87.8	0.1
Kindergarten teachers	1.1	98.9	0.0

Source: Kajima 1995, 5.

Breaking down managerial positions by types of occupations, in the Kyrgyz Republic females account for about half of the managers in three types of occupations: trade (54 percent), education (51 percent), and health and social protection (48 percent), but they remain a low proportion at between 15 and 30 percent in all other types of occupations such as industry, agriculture, transport and construction, and government administration (Bauer, Green, and Kuehnast 1997, 30). This seems to suggest that women have higher chances of development in the social sector, whereas the technical, specialist, and government administrative positions are still dominated by men.

However, in some DMCs professional and managerial occupations are clearly male empires. The Lao PDR is an example. Unskilled and laboring jobs are largely undertaken by women (with a male/female ratio of about 1:2.5), while professional and managerial jobs are largely dominated by men, with men outnumbering women by 20 times (Table 16).

Gender disparity in wages is also clear. Apart from service and farm jobs, men's wages are 1.2 to 2 times higher than women's in nearly all kinds of occupations (see Appendix 1, Table A1.3); and men's advantage over females in wages occurs across all levels of education (see Appendix 1, Table A1.4). According to UNDP figures in 1998, in most DMCs, women's share of earned income is only 25 to 40 percent (see Appendix 1, Table A1.5). Given that women in general account for 35 to 45 percent of the adult labor force (see also Table 11), there is an obvious gender disparity in wages. In Hong Kong, China, females exceed males among the lower income working population and among unpaid family workors, but the pattern is reversed among the upper-income population across all education levels (see Appendix 1, Table A1.6). Nonetheless, according to figures from Indonesia, despite disparity in wages, the impact of additional schooling on earnings is higher for females than for males. This means that education is still an important key for females to enhance their life chances and earnings (see Appendix 1, Table A1.7).

Table 16: Employment by Occupation and Gender in the Lao PDR, 1992 and 1994

Occupation	1992			1994		
	M%	F%	M/F	M%	F%	M/F
Administrator/Manager	2.58	0.13	19.8	3.07	0.35	8.8
Professional/Scientific worker	8.93	6.99	1.3	8.34	3.94	2.1
Technician	2.07	1.87	1.1	13.68	20.09	0.7
Clerk	10.61	4.65	2.3	12.03	11.90	1.0
Service worker	0.77	2.14	0.4	3.03	5.02	0.6
Farm worker	38.90	46.93	0.8	5.49	4.82	1.1
Craft and related trades/Skilled worker	18.56	10.48	1.8	12.18	8.22	1.5
Semi-skilled worker	5.80	0.28	20.7	—	—	—
Unskilled worker	11.78	26.53	0.4	—	—	—
Plant and machine operator	—	—	—	13.62	4.98	2.7
Elementary occupation	—	—	—	20.96	35.91	0.6
Armed forces	—	—	—	3.89	0.40	9.7
Not stated	—	—	—	3.71	4.36	0.9

— Data not available.

Source: Netherlands Economic Institute 1995, 17, 48.

Women still seem to have little influence in social and political decisions. Not only do women in general account for a low proportion of administrative and managerial positions that involve everyday decisions at the microscopic social level; at the macroscopic government level, women are still a clear minority. Looking at gender distribution in government, women in most DMCs constitute below 5 percent of ministerial or subministerial positions. The few exceptions are Philippines (23 percent), Fiji Islands (15 percent), and Maldives (13 percent). Even taking into account these few countries with more women representatives, at the maximum they hold only one quarter of positions at subministerial level. They are still a clear minority in the government body (see Appendix 1, Table A1.8). It is therefore worth noting that the GEM values in DMCs are all lower than the GDI values (Table 1).

Policy Implications

From the above analysis, eight major policy implications emerge. These are presented below.

(i) *Population control and increase of school places.* The size of the illiterate population has not been reduced over the last 20 years. This suggests the need for strategies to enhance access to education. First is the old but still significant issue of population control, which remains a major agenda item for many DMCs. Where the school-aged population is growing rapidly (India 2.1 percent, Nepal 2.3 percent, Bangladesh 2.7 percent, Mongolia 2.7 percent, Lao PDR 2.8 percent, Pakistan 2.9 percent, and Afghanistan 4.8 percent), school places may have to be doubled within 20 years to maintain today's enrollment rates. The same increase takes over 70 years with a 1 percent annual increase rate (Lewin 1996, 32, 61). Family planning and various other types of intersectoral planning affecting population growth are crucial to the delivery of education.

(ii) *Increasing education for females should be a priority.* Given that the growth of the illiterate population is obviously attributable to the increase of female illiterates, enhancing education opportunities for females should be a priority. UNESCO (1996, 20) argues that enrollments for girls should be "the priority of priorities." It is widely pointed out that returns from education are higher for females than for males, and that there is a positive correlation between the education of females and poverty reduction, improved health, nutrition of women, and reduced fertility rates (ADB 1994b, 23; Todaro 1997, 383).

(iii) *Enhancing retention rates should be a priority in primary schooling.* Measures to retain children in schools should be a priority for many DMCs, especially those in South Asia. This is important both to improve access and equity in education, and to enhance internal efficiency in education investment. For example, the ADB report (1996e, 13) on human development in Viet Nam estimates that if measures are not taken to reduce dropouts and repeaters, Viet Nam would require 37,000 additional classes,

18,000 additional classrooms, 41,000 extra teachers, an extra $131 million in capital costs, and $75 million to $90 million in recurrent costs by 2010. Chuard and Mingat's (1996b) study of dropouts in South Asia shows that repetition can be a cause for dropping out. Their study also identifies a number of factors that may be related to dropouts, which have significant implications for policymakers:

(a) *Preschooling* helps achieve higher levels of learning in primary education, even up to Grade 4. The logical policy implication is to encourage preschooling, but this will cause dilemmas for low-income countries as preschooling is very costly.

(b) *Improving the quality of teachers* is important, as students whose teacher ratings were better had a significantly higher probability of not dropping out.

(c) *The school factor* is significant in retaining students. Surveys found that:

- large schools may be able to achieve better learning outcomes;
- complete schools are crucial to retain students when they see that higher grades are available in the school;
- good multigrade teaching has a positive impact on learning, and helps implement the policy of complete schools;
- providing food for students has a positive influence on school outcomes, both in terms of learning and student retention; and
- running large classes is not counter to learning outcomes, and teacher training can incorporate techniques of how to manage classes of 50 or 60 students (Chuard and Mingat 1996b, 31; Mingat and Chuard 1996, 59).

(iv) *Specific programs and measures are required to reduce repetition and dropout of children already attending schools.* These programs may include awareness programs for students concerning the significance of schooling, medical programs to ensure student health, school textbook rental programs to enhance accessibility of learning materials, and reforms in curriculum and pedagogy to allow students to understand fully their lessons, etc. Further, to enhance retention, a number of policies need to be considered, in view of the discussions above, such as placing the best teachers in early grades to give children a good start, parental involvement, community participation, peer tutoring, and reducing absenteeism of teachers and students.

(v) *Primary education must remain a priority in development.* Primary education is still a priority in development that cannot be bypassed (Chuard and Mingat, 1996b, 3). Concerning Nepal, Bajracharya, Thapa, and Chitrakar (1997, 40) point out that most external assistance has been provided for technical and higher education. They indicate that the significance of re-emphasizing investments in primary education has begun to be realized, and has to be consolidated. However, at present it seems that there is more rhetoric than action in reinstating primary education, especially when considering the higher investments in secondary, tertiary, and vocational/technical education.

(vi) *Development programs need to be more gender-specific.* When presenting policies on gender equity, it is common for governments to justify equity by legislative availability of equal or open access to education and employment. However, if women are a disadvantaged group, such gender-neutral policies can only be regarded as a passive measure (McDonald 1995, 55). Not only is such a passive measure not helpful for females, it sometimes produces negative effects. ADB (1994b, 1) points out that:

> ... it became increasingly clear that the rewards and benefits of development had not always been distributed and shared equally by males and females. Development projects in some instances had either ignored women altogether or marginalized them, while in other instances, projects may have resulted in negative consequences for women such as an increase in their workload, diminished access to fuelwood, depletion and pollution of water sources, domestic violence and decreased control over traditionally inherited land. Rather than enhancing women's economic, social, and political status, development activities have sometimes reinforced existing gender inequalities, or generated and promoted new forms and patterns of discrimination against women.

Gender-specific measures to enhance females' access to education may include:

- affirmative measures to increase the proportion of females given studentships and scholarships;
- awareness campaigns for girls' enrollments, recruitment of female teachers, and increased access for girls; and
- concentration on gender parity in teaching, managing, and policy making.

(vii) *Different priorities for different levels of schooling.* While consolidating primary education, there are certainly pressures to increase enrollments in secondary and tertiary education. Efforts should certainly be made to increase enrollments at the secondary level, as well as increasing retention and reducing repetition. How much expansion should be sought for the tertiary sector remains a complicated issue. However, in terms of equity and access, it is obvious that:

- *Rationalization of expenditure distribution across the three levels of education* needs to be sorted out, as the small proportion of students studying at the tertiary level enjoy a large proportion of education resources. One possible solution for governments is to provide basic education largely free or at highly subsidized rates, and leave higher education to the private sector so that those who can afford the high fees have to pay (with the provision of scholarships for those who cannot afford, on a merit basis) (see ADB 1995, 28).

- *Increasing female participation in secondary and tertiary education* should be a significant item. While gender parity in primary enrollment seems to be less of an issue in most DMCs, as the review above shows, in about half the DMCs boys' enrollments exceed girls' by 1.1 to 2.9 times in secondary education, and by 1.1 to 3 times in tertiary education, with a few even up to 5.4 times.

- *The specific tasks for the different levels of education* seem to be improving the quality of primary education and its internal efficiency (in terms of reducing repetitions and dropouts) when primary education is almost universal; aiming at universalization of lower secondary education for most DMCs; and enhancing female enrollments in both secondary and tertiary education.

- *Vocational and technical education needs more studies.* Such education is more emphasized in some countries and less in others within DMCs, but how far this should be expanded or strengthened requires more detailed examination. Taipei,China used to have 70 percent of upper secondary students enrolled in vocational and technical education, and the PRC had a target of reaching a 50:50 ratio of academic to vocational and technical streams at upper secondary level. However, the former has begun to cut down the proportion of the vocational and technical stream, while the latter varies in ratio by region. Governments need to be cautious about overinvestment in vocational and technical education, as it may not be able to fit a fast-growing economy when the requirements of new techniques emerge faster than formal schooling can offer (see Bray 2002).

- *A cautionary note is needed on the consolidation of primary education and expansion of secondary education.* In addition to the retention of primary students, and as a part of strategies to achieve the goal, attention should be paid to the extent to which students actually receive second class primary education in the process of its universalization, especially girls. It is quite common that the speed of universalizing education is achieved by providing extensive schools with insufficient facilities and underqualified teachers. This may cause another form of inequity.

(viii) *Helping women help women.* Women's groups have been active for a long time, but they need the opportunity to develop their organizational, management, programming, and technical skills. Training opportunities for staff in nongovernment organizations (NGOs) in these areas should be more widely available. Projects are needed to improve the organizational and management capacity of women's NGOs in order to equip them to run more efficiently and effectively (Emberson-Bain 1995, 57).

Box 1: The Primacy of Primary Education

The advanced Asian economies emphasized primary education at a very early stage of their development, before they entered the high-growth phase. For instance, in 1960, just before the high-growth phase, these economies had enrollment rates of 4 to 10 percent in higher education but already had nearly universal primary enrollment.

The effectiveness of this strategy is demonstrated by high retention rates in schools, higher learning achievements than even the OECD countries, and the robust statistical association between primary-level enrollment rates and subsequent high growth. This evidence reinforces the conclusions of earlier studies that have demonstrated the high rates of return from primary education and its positive impact on labor productivity, health, and other social objectives.

These conclusions suggest that the prioritization of different levels of education services in many DMCs today is quite the opposite of the priorities that may be necessary for education to serve as an effective instrument for promoting either equity or rapid economic growth.

Source: ADB 1995, 22-3.

Income-Related Equity

South Asia and Sub-Saharan Africa together have the highest incidence of income poverty (by the $1-a-day poverty line) in the world. In terms of proportion, the incidence of income poverty in South Asia is 43 percent. In terms of number, South Asia is home to one third (515 million of 1.3 billion) of the income poor. East Asia, South Asia, Southeast Asia, and the Pacific together account for 960 million of the 1.3 billion income poor (UNDP 1997, 47). The proportion of income poor in less developed countries declined only slightly from 34 percent in 1987 to 32 percent in 1993, but the number of income poor increased from 1.2 billion to 1.3 billion. In general, the proportion of the income poor declined rather slowly in East and South Asia. But the "big five" in Asia, namely, Bangladesh, the PRC, India, Indonesia, and Pakistan, made impressive progress in reducing income poverty (UNDP 1997, 33).

Income Distribution and Equality

Looking at the ratio of the income share of the top quintile to that of the bottom quintile in three groups of Asian economies (Table 17), the NIEs (7.0) have the lowest value compared with countries in the Association of Southeast Asian Nations (ASEAN) and South Asia. However, the ASEAN countries have the highest value (10.6), indicating that they are more unequal in income distribution than the higher-income NIEs and the lower-income South Asian countries. Taipei,China has the most equitable income distribution – better even than some countries outside the region such as Hungary (5.2) and Yugoslavia (5.9). Among the NIEs, income distribution is particularly unequal

Box 2: Poverty and Illiteracy in Bangladesh

Bangladesh, with a 1994 GNP per capita of just $230, is a very low-income country. The figure makes Bangladesh the 12th poorest among countries with at least 1 million population, even though at purchasing power parity the income becomes PPP$1,350 with a similar ranking. The country is the largest among those poorer than the PRC and India: 119 million people live in Bangladesh.

Life expectancy is 55 years in Bangladesh. Illiteracy is high, at 78 percent of adult women and 65 percent of adult men. The infant mortality rate is 108 per 1,000. The Government places 50 percent, and the United Nations 85 percent, of the population below the poverty line.

Source: Todaro 1997, 412.

Table 17: Percentage Share of Household Income by Quintile Group in Selected Asian Countries, 1970s and 1980s

	Year	Bottom 20% Q1 (%)	Second quintile Q2 (%)	Third quintile Q3 (%)	Fourth quintile Q4 (%)	Top 20% Q5 (%)	Q5/Q1
NIEs		6.6	12.1	16.2	21.7	43.5	7.0
Hong Kong, China	1980	5.4	10.8	15.2	21.6	47.0	8.7
Korea, Republic of	1976	5.7	11.2	15.4	22.4	45.3	7.9
Singapore	1973	6.4	12.4	16.5	20.0	44.7	7.0
Taipei,China	1980	8.8	13.9	17.7	22.8	36.8	4.2
ASEAN		5.2	8.5	13.0	21.3	52.0	10.6
Indonesia	1976	6.6	7.8	12.6	23.6	49.4	7.5
Malaysia	1973	3.5	7.7	12.4	20.3	56.1	16.0
Philippines	1985	5.2	8.9	13.2	20.2	52.5	10.1
Thailand	1975/76	5.6	9.6	13.9	21.1	49.8	8.9
South Asia		6.0	9.5	13.8	19.9	50.9	8.8
Bangladesh	1981/82	6.6	10.7	15.3	22.1	45.3	6.9
India	1975/76	7.0	9.2	13,9	20.5	49.4	7.1
Nepal	1976/77	4.6	8.0	11.7	16.5	59.2	12.9
Sri Lanka	1980/81	5.8	10.1	14.1	20.3	49.8	8.6

Source: Extracted from Bautista 1990, 6, Table 2.

in Hong Kong, China. Among the four ASEAN countries shown, Thailand and Indonesia have achieved a degree of income distribution close to that of the NIEs, while Malaysia has the greatest income equality in the region. In South Asia, the degree of income distribution is close to that of the NIEs, except that Nepal's situation is close to that of Malaysia and the Philippines; Bangladesh's is close to Singapore's.

Gini coefficients show extreme variations within Asia. Figures in the 1980s showed that the Gini index of most DMCs varied between 30 and 40. A few achieved very low income disparities, such as Republic of Korea (15.9), Philippines (18.6), and Indonesia (27.3). Countries with high income disparities included the PRC (44.4), Nepal (57.9), Papua New Guinea (62.1), and India (65.8); Bangladesh's index was as high as 81.9. The years following the mid-1980s brought a decline in income disparity in some DMCs: between 1985 and 1996 Nepal dropped from 57.9 to 36.7, India from 65.8 to 29.7, and Bangladesh substantially from 81.9 to 28.3. However, some DMCs witnessed widening income disparity, such as the Philippines where the Gini index increased from 18.6 in 1985 to 42.9 in 1996 (Table 18), and Hong Kong, China, where it rose from 37.7 in 1971 to 42.1 in 1991. Figures for Hong Kong, China in 1991 also showed that the inequality of income distribution of working men (42.4) was higher than that of working women (38.3) (Lui 1997, 46, 54).

The growth in income inequality seems to be related to economic liberalization and growth. For example, in the PRC, the Gini index was 33 in 1979, which was lower than that in any other East Asian country. However, after a decade of economic liberalization and growth, the Gini index rose to 42, which was higher than those of Indonesia and the Republic of Korea. Inequality continues to rise in the PRC, especially along the coast (UNDP 1996, 59).

Table 18: Gini Index in Selected DMCs

Country	1985	1996[a,b]
Cambodia	—	51.3
Papua New Guinea	62.1	50.9
Malaysia	37.9	48.4
Thailand	32.9	46.2
Philippines	18.6	42.9
China, People's Republic of	44.4	41.5
Nepal	57.9	36.7
Indonesia	27.3	36.5
Viet Nam	—	35.7
Kyrgyz Republic	—	35.3
Mongolia	—	33.2
Kazakhstan	—	32.7
Pakistan	—	31.2
Lao People's Democratic Republic	—	30.4
Sri Lanka	32.6	30.1
India	65.8	29.7
Bangladesh	81.9	28.3
Korea, Republic of	15.9	—

— Data not available.
[a] Data refer to the most recent year available.
[b] Table is sorted by this column heading.

Sources: Gertler and Rahman 1994, 168; Krongkaew, Tinakorn, and Suphachalasai 1996, 607, 612; World Bank 1999, 70-2.

Capability Poverty

UNDP (1997, 16) advocates a capability perspective on poverty. This reconciles the notions of absolute and relative poverty, since relative deprivation in incomes and commodities can lead to an absolute deprivation in minimum capabilities. In 1996, UNDP introduced a multidimensional index of human deprivation known as the Capability Poverty Measure (CPM), as distinguished from income poverty. The CPM considers the lack of three basic capabilities, namely nourishment and health, healthy reproduction, and education, particularly in relation to female literacy. The UNDP observes that in most countries in South Asia, capability poverty is more widespread than income poverty. In Pakistan, only one third of the population is income poor, but three fifths are capability poor. In Bangladesh, 55 million people are income poor but 89 million are capability poor. In Sri Lanka, by contrast, capability poverty is less than income poverty. Thailand has been successful in reducing capability poverty to a level lower than income poverty, but it is the other way round in Indonesia (Table 19).

Referring to capability poverty and education, Tilak's analysis shows a clear positive relationship between poverty and illiteracy in Asia, i.e., the higher the percentage of poverty in a country, the lower the literacy rate (Figure 2).

In Indonesia, there is an obvious difference in enrollment rates between the poor and the nonpoor. In 1987, among the 7-12 age group, net enrollment rates (NERs) were close to 90 percent for both the poor (87.3 percent) and

Table 19: Capability Poverty and Income Poverty in Selected DMCs, 1993 (percent)

Country	Population: capability poor	Population: income poor
Bangladesh	76.9	47.5
China, People's Republic of	17.5	10.9
India	61.5	25.4
Indonesia	42.3	16.7
Pakistan	60.8	34.0
Sri Lanka	19.3	22.4
Thailand	21.1	21.8

Source: UNDP 1996, 27.

Figure 2: Literacy and Poverty in Asia

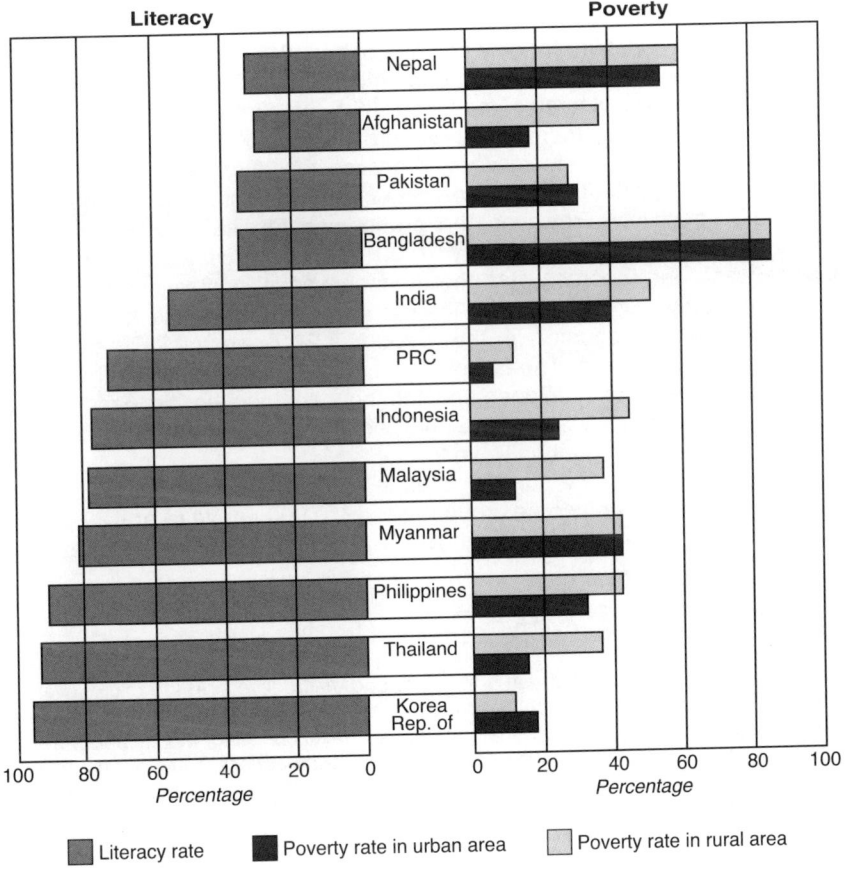

Source: Tilak 1994, 122.

the nonpoor (93.2 percent). However, as the children grew older, the gap became wider. Among the 13-15 age group, the NERs of the poor dropped to 58.4 percent, whereas the rates of the nonpoor dropped to 78.2 percent. Among the 16-18 age group, the rates of the poor dropped to 21.1 percent, whereas the nonpoor dropped to 52.8 percent. Thus while 90 percent of poor and nonpoor children get access to primary school, entry to senior secondary education is achieved by only one fifth of the poor, but half of the nonpoor. Accordingly, the illiteracy rates of the poor are higher than those of the nonpoor, and the difference between the poor and nonpoor among the older school age group is much wider than the other age groups. Illiteracy among the poor is two to three times that of the nonpoor (Table 20).

The gap between the poor and the nonpoor is also obvious in the Lao PDR. The NERs of the poorest are only half of the richest at the primary level; and their access to junior secondary education is significantly limited, with NER as low as 4 percent. Likewise, while illiterates account for half of the poorest age groups, they account for only one fifth of the 18-35 age group and even as low as 9 percent of the 35-55 age group among the richest (Table 21).

In Bangladesh, illiterates make up 85.5 percent of the poorest adult population, and 63.6 percent of the moderately poor population, but only 47.0 percent of the nonpoor. In respect of access to education, among the age group of 6-15, only 52.8 and 43.0 percent of the poorest are male and female students respectively. However, the proportions for the nonpoor male and female populations are respectively 70.0 and 61.8 percent. There is a large gap between the poorest and the nonpoor adult population with higher education. Only 9.7 percent of the poorest literate adults attain higher education, but the proportion for the nonpoor is 24.7 percent, i.e., nearly three times that of the poorest. The Bangladesh figures show that apart from a gap in enrollment between the poor and the nonpoor, females in general have lower enrollment rates than males, and poor females are obviously the most deprived group in the country (Table 22).

In the Philippines, the survival rates in primary education varied between 57 percent of the lower-income group (below P10,000 per year) and 89 percent of the higher-income group (above P30,000 per year) in 1982. In

Box 3: Education and Poverty

Education is related to poverty at both micro and macro levels. At the micro level, illiterate individuals or households are less productive, join lower-paying occupations, and thus earn less and remain at very low levels of living, mostly below the poverty line. At the macro level, nations with illiterate or less educated masses cannot progress well, cannot increase their output substantially, and as a result remain with low standards of living. The impact of the relationship between poverty and education is further felt as education and other basic needs reinforce each other. Less educated households and nations are also characterized by high mortality rates and poor health.

Source: Tilak 1994, 115.

Table 20: Net Enrollment Rates and Illiteracy Rates of Poor and Nonpoor in Indonesia, 1987
(percent)

	Net enrollment rates			Illiteracy rates		
Group	Age 7-12	Age 13-15	Age 16-18	Age 7-13	Age 14-29	Age over 29
Poor	87.3	58.4	21.1	20.1	16.3	49.7
Nonpoor	93.2	78.2	52.8	12.4	5.6	30.1

Source: World Bank figures, cited in Tjondronegoro, Soejono, and Hardjono 1996, 211, 213.

Table 21: Net Enrollment Rates and Illiteracy Rates by Income Quintiles in the Lao PDR, 1993
(percent)

	Net enrollment rates		Illiteracy rates	
Income Quintiles	Primary	Junior secondary	Age 18-35	Age 35-55
Poorest	44	4	54	43
II	50	10	49	36
III	61	14	39	23
IV	68	18	39	20
Richest	78	28	23	9

Source: Chagnon 1996, 40, 42.

Table 22: Education and Literacy of Poor and Nonpoor Households in Bangladesh, 1987/88
(percent)

	Extremely poor	Moderately poor	Non-poor
Age group 6-15 as students: Male	52.8	63.0	70.0
Age group 6-15 as students: Female	43.0	56.5	61.8
Illiterate adult members	85.5	63.6	47.0
Literate adult members with higher education	9.7	14.4	24.7

Source: Hossain, Mannab, Rahman, and Sen 1994, 110.

other words, the chance of school completion of children in the higher-income group was nearly twice that of the lower-income group (Gertler and Rahman 1994, 155). Quibria (1996, 35) points out that although there is an almost 100 percent enrollment of children aged between 7 and 10, the rate drops after that age, particularly among the poor. The quality of schooling in primary and secondary public schools, especially in rural areas, is weak. Tilak (1994, 120) comments that an increase in rural employment in the Philippines is confined to the agriculture sector and to a small percentage of the poor. Also, the spread of the benefits of growth is mainly confined to rich farmers. The lack of political will explains the poor progress of the country in the reduction of poverty and income inequalities.

In the Republic of Korea, enrollment rates in middle school, high school, and university/college were 100 percent, 88.9 percent, and 37.5 percent among the rural nonpoor; but were 93.8 percent, 40.0 percent, and 0 percent among the rural poor (Chung and Oh 1996, 329). In Viet Nam, the NERs of the richest 20 percent of the population decline from 86 percent to 56 percent, 28 percent, and 7 percent accordingly from primary level, to junior secondary level, senior secondary level, and post-secondary level. However, the decline in NERs of the poorest 20 percent is from 68 percent, to 19 percent, 2 percent, and 0 percent respectively (ADB 1996e, 3). Enrollment rates in the Republic of Korea are generally higher than those in Viet Nam, but equally the rural poor in the Republic of Korea and the poorest 20 percent in Viet Nam have little access to higher education.

Financial Burdens on the Poor: Fees and Household Expenditures

While primary education in Asia is officially free of charge, in many countries unofficial fees are demanded at the secondary level (Bray 1996, 17). Also, all sorts of unofficial levies have put financial burdens upon parents at all levels. In some countries, such as Viet Nam, where post-primary schooling used to be free of charge, fees have been introduced because of economic stringency. An ADB report on human development in Viet Nam points out that the introduction of user charges is an access barrier for poor families in education. The costs of primary school textbooks and incidentals, which are around 83,000 dong per pupil, cannot be met by the poorer families. Forty percent of rural households indicate that excessive costs are the main reason for nonattendance at primary schools. In 1994, the NER of the poorest quintile was 67.7 percent, and the rates rose to 77.3 percent, 80.7 percent, 84.7 percent, and 86.2 percent to the richest quintile (ADB 1996e, 13).

Bray's (1996, 40-1) study of parental and community financing of education in East Asia also notes that in various parts of Asia, a substantial proportion of household incomes is spent on education: 3.3 percent of household incomes in Phnom Penh, Cambodia (1993/94); 29 percent of household incomes in the poorest part, 19 percent in middle-income parts, and 14 percent in rich parts in Guangdong, PRC (1994); 38 percent of per capita incomes in the poorest quintile and 17 percent in the richest quintile in Indonesia (1989); 6.1 percent of nonfood household expenditure in Mongolia (1995); 15.6 percent of average family incomes in Myanmar (1990); 46.7 percent of household incomes in terms of opportunity costs for the poorest and 1.9 percent for the top income group in the Philippines (1987); and 22.0 percent of nonfood consumption per primary student for direct costs among the poorest quintile in Viet Nam (1993). The opportunity costs for education are exceptionally high among the poorest quintile, but low among the richest quintile. This means that the financial pressure on families to support their children for education is still substantial among the poor in DMCs.

The issue of opportunity cost arises in relatively prosperous societies as well as impoverished ones. In the high-growth provinces of the Philippines, the problem of "low payoff, high opportunity cost" creates dropouts from secondary schools among the poor (World Bank 1996b, 115). The pressure on enrollments resulting from fast economic development is also notable in the PRC. For some years since the opening up of the economy, the notion that "education is useless" has been held in fast-developing economic regions such as Guangdong, because people see faster rates of return in direct employment than in investment in education. Only when the economy has grown to such an extent that it requires more qualified human resources will people begin to look for attainment in higher education for a higher level job (Hook and Lee, 1998).

Policy Implications

The relationships between education, poverty, and income inequalities are complex. In a nutshell, while poverty is a hindrance to attaining education, education is the means to break through poverty. Gertler and Rahman (1994, 129) remark that improving the human capital of the poor will not only redress these inequalities but may also help reduce economic poverty. Tilak (1994, 119-20) has identified a number of DMCs that have made substantial investments in human capital with resulting benefits of growth and reduction of poverty. For example, the Republic of Korea – where growth and equity went together – making education accessible to all citizens contributed significantly to increasing the supply of skilled and technical human resources in the short run, and to equitable income distribution in the long run. Although emphasizing growth more than social welfare, the Republic of Korea has spent large amounts on education and other social welfare programs.

Of course, much private and household money is part of the education investment, especially at the higher education level. Malaysia and Thailand have also pursued heavy investment in human capital and encouraged efficient labor-intensive growth in agriculture and industry, resulting in an obvious reduction of inequality. In Sri Lanka, decline in poverty and a reduction in inequality were the results of welfare state policies. Even under severe economic conditions, public subsidies in education and health have remained priorities in investment.

These remarks may lead to the following policy considerations:

(i) *Population control and basic education should remain a priority.* The need for population control and basic education was highlighted above. This need is emphasized by the fact that although the proportion of the income poor has declined, their number has increased, and the poor, especially poor females, are vulnerable to school nonattendance and noncompletion.

(ii) *Government intervention is required to ensure access by the poor.* Todaro's remarks in Box 4 are noteworthy: compared with the rich, (i) the private costs of primary education are a greater burden for the poor, (ii) the expected benefits of primary education are lower for the income poor, (iii) the opportunity costs of labor are higher, and (iv) children of the poor are seldom able to proceed beyond the first few years of schooling. All these stress the need for government intervention to ensure access of the poor to resources and education facilities. Walton (1990, 4) points out that the effectiveness of national development strategies is strongly influenced by the extent to which public policy and intervention take

Box 4: Education, Inequality, and Poverty

There are two fundamental economic reasons why one might suspect that many less developed countries' education systems are inherently inegalitarian, in the sense that poor students have less chance of completing any given education cycle than more affluent students. First, the private costs of primary education (especially in view of the opportunity costs of child labor to poor families) are higher for poor students than for more affluent students. Second, the expected benefits of primary education are lower for poor students. Together, the higher costs and lower expected benefits of education mean that a poor family's rate of return from investment in a child's education is lower than it is for other families. The poor are therefore more likely to drop out during the early years of schooling.

Elaborating on this point, the higher opportunity costs of labor to poor families means that even if the first few years of education are free, they are not without cost to the family. Children of primary school age are typically needed to work on family farms, often at the same time as they are required to be at school. If children cannot work because they are at school, the families either suffer a loss of valuable subsistence output or are required to hire paid labor. In either case, there is a real cost to a poor family of having an able-bodied child attend school when there is productive work to be done on the farm – a cost not related to tuition and of much less significance to higher-income families, many of whom live in urban areas where child work is not needed.

As a result of these high opportunity costs, school attendance, and therefore school performance, tends to be much lower for the children of poor families than for those from higher-income backgrounds. Thus in spite of the existence of free and universal primary education in many countries, children of the poor are seldom able to proceed beyond the first few years of schooling. Their weak school performance may have nothing to do with a lack of cognitive abilities: it may merely reflect their disadvantaged economic circumstances.

Source: Todaro 1997, 396.

account of the needs and circumstances of the poor and involve them in the design and implementation of programs. Success in poverty reduction has everywhere been associated with a combination of creating income-earning opportunities for the poor and strong support for human resource development.

(iii) *The efficiency of government subsidies in redistributing income should be improved.* Government subsidies are available in most countries for social services, including education. However, usually these subsidies are more accessible to the nonpoor. For example, public schools and health care facilities tend to be located in cities and are closer to the nonpoor. Even when facing the same accessibility of services and facilities, the nonpoor tend to use these services and facilities more than the poor due to better awareness of the services and income effects. Since government subsidies per student increase significantly with increased level of education, those who manage to stay longest in the education system, who are usually the rich, can enjoy larger shares of public subsidies to education. This suggests that government social and education subsidies are not well enough targeted and therefore not efficient at redistributing income (Gertler and Rahman 1994, 139, 153). For example, Lucas and Verry (1996, 570) observe that the expansion of tertiary education in the 1980s in Malaysia actually benefited the relatively wealthy within each community rather than the poor, and recommend that upgrading the quality of basic education, especially in rural areas where poverty is concentrated, might reduce the unequal distribution of income more directly. To realize targeted education welfare for the poor, corresponding measures may include the following:

- Open new facilities, including schools, closer to households in need, so as to reduce access costs, and improve the quality of schooling inputs.
- Pro-poor biased subsidies can be adopted, such as channeling all or the largest share of subsidies to primary education and lower secondary education. However, care should be taken to avoid subsidies to higher education becoming pro-rich, which can easily offset the pro-poor policy.
- Subsidies may be targeted, e.g., through scholarships and stipends, rather than made indiscriminate e.g., through general subsidization in the form of low fees in higher education. The need to discriminate in distribution of direct subsidies assumes that subsidies in the form of scholarships can change private and social rates of return substantially, and can even change the relative rank order of the rates of return according to different groups of population (Tilak 1994, 131).
- School construction activities and the suspension of fees for poor families may be necessary to help them to attend school. There has been successful experience in Indonesia, for example (Tilak 1994, 118).
- Food-for-Education programs may encourage retention and improve the health of children in poor families. Some successes have been reported in Bangladesh, for example (Mingat and Chuard 1996, 79).

Box 5: Government Measures to Reduce Poverty in the Republic of Korea

The role of the government is important in ensuring the welfare of the poor, because it is unlikely that the private sector will take over this role totally. For this reason, the Government of the Republic of Korea implements various assistance policies.

The poverty reduction programs include ones to enlarge employment opportunities and to provide social security benefits. Among them are medical insurance and health care, national pensions, industrial accident insurance, and minimum wages. A livelihood assistance system assists the poor directly, and includes medical aid, tuition fee assistance, vocational training, and long-term low-interest loans.

Source: Chang 1991, 18.

Region-Related Equity

Region-related disparity is of two major kinds: urban-rural disparity and regional disparity within countries. Each of these is considered here in turn. This section also presents a case study of the PRC, comments on the scale and nature of urban poverty, and identifies policy implications.

Urban-Rural Disparities

Tables 23-28 show that literacy and enrollment rates are in general higher in urban regions across countries and over time. Gender, income, and regional equity problems are often closely related to one another. This means that rural poor females are the most vulnerable group. For example in Afghanistan, Nepal, and Pakistan, the literacy rates for males in urban regions were about twice those in rural regions in 1980. For females, the rates were respectively 9.5 times, 4.3 times, and 5.3 times those of rural regions in these countries (Table 23).

The gap in school completion rates is also wide. Referring to the rate of secondary school completion in DMCs, Table 24 shows that in 1980 the completion rates of males in urban areas were three to five times those of their rural counterparts. Whereas the completion rates of females in urban areas were three to ten times those of their rural counterparts, the urban/rural

Table 23: Literacy Rates by Region and Gender in Selected DMCs, 1970s and 1980s

| | Circa 1970 | | | | | | Circa 1980 | | | | | |
| | Male | | | Female | | | Male | | | Female | | |
Country	U %	R %	U/R	U %	R %	U/R	U %	R %	U/R	U %	R %	U/R
Afghanistan	43.8	18.7	2.3	16.5	0.6	27.5	52.3	26.3	2.0	20.8	2.2	9.5
Bangladesh	57.9	34.6	1.7	33.2	11.5	2.9	58.0	35.5	1.6	34.1	15.3	2.2
India	72.4	40.6	1.8	45.5	13.0	3.5	76.4	47.3	1.6	51.9	17.6	2.9
Indonesia	87.7	65.5	1.3	66.2	40.1	1.7	91.1	73.2	1.2	75.9	52.2	1.5
Korea, Rep. of	98.0	91.5	1.1	90.7	73.4	1.2	—	—	—	—	—	—
Malaysia	80.1	64.1	1.2	55.3	36.8	1.5	88.1	74.3	1.2	72.0	53.0	1.4
Nepal	73.4	26.1	2.8	27.4	2.3	11.9	59.7	29.6	2.0	33.0	7.6	4.3
Pakistan	50.1	22.0	2.3	28.9	4.2	6.9	56.9	26.6	2.1	35.9	6.8	5.3
Philippines	94.0	79.6	1.2	91.3	75.3	1.2	94.1	77.6	1.2	92.3	76.1	1.2
Sri Lanka	90.6	85.1	1.1	80.3	65.1	1.2	95.6	89.3	1.1	90.8	78.6	1.2
Thailand	93.7	86.1	1.1	81.9	68.4	1.2	—	—	—	—	—	—

— Data not available.
U = Urban population; R = Rural population; U/R = Urban/Rural ratio.
Note: Data refer to population 15 years old and over.

Source: ADB 1993, 140-5.

Table 24: Population that has Completed Secondary School by Region and Gender, Selected DMCs, 1970s-1990s

Country	Circa 1970 Male U%	R%	U/R	Female U%	R%	U/R	Circa 1980 Male U%	R%	U/R	Female U%	R%	U/R	Latest Male U%	R%	U/R	Female U%	R%	U/R
Korea, Rep. of	26.6	11.9	2.2	14.6	2.6	5.6	41.5	22.1	1.9	26.7	7.7	3.5	39.8	26.8	1.5	32.3	13.1	2.5
Indonesia	13.6	1.8	7.6	9.0	0.5	18.0	21.4	4.3	5.0	11.9	1.7	7.0	32.0	7.2	4.4	18.6	3.0	6.2
Malaysia	—	—	—	—	—	—	4.9	1.7	2.9	2.9	0.8	3.6	—	—	—	—	—	—
Philippines	15.8	4.4	3.6	10.6	2.3	4.6	—	—	—	—	—	—	—	—	—	—	—	—
Viet Nam	—	—	—	—	—	—	—	—	—	—	—	—	20.3	4.3	4.7	15.2	2.8	5.4
Afghanistan	6.6	1.6	4.1	2.6	—	—	—	—	—	—	—	—	—	—	—	—	—	—
Bangladesh	—	—	—	—	—	—	16.4	5.1	3.2	5.7	0.6	9.5	—	—	—	—	—	—
India	17.0	4.6	3.7	7.1	0.6	11.8	37.1	8.6	4.3	17.8	1.7	10.5	—	—	—	—	—	—
Nepal	—	—	—	—	—	—	23.4	6.1	3.8	10.9	0.7	15.6	—	—	—	—	—	—
Pakistan	—	—	—	—	—	—	38.8	6.2	6.3	32.1	0.7	45.9	—	—	—	—	—	—
Sri Lanka	2.2	1.5	1.5	2.1	1.2	1.8	—	—	—	—	—	—	—	—	—	—	—	—
Vanuatu	—	—	—	—	—	—	8.2	1.7	4.8	—	—	—	—	—	—	—	—	—

— Data not available.
U = Urban population; R = Rural population; U/R = Urban/Rural ratio.
Note: Data refer to population 20 years old and over.

Source: ADB 1993, 152-7.

Table 25: Population of University Graduates by Region and Gender in Selected DMCs, 1970s-1990s

Country	Circa 1970 Male U%	R%	U/R	Female U%	R%	U/R	Circa 1980 Male U%	R%	U/R	Female U%	R%	U/R	Latest Male U%	R%	U/R	Female U%	R%	U/R
Korea, Rep. of	12.7	2.0	6.4	2.6	0.2	13.0	16.1	3.1	5.2	4.9	0.5	9.8	16.9	4.1	4.1	5.7	0.9	6.3
Indonesia	3.0	0.2	15.0	0.9	—	—	5.0	0.5	10.0	2.1	0.2	10.5	5.3	0.7	7.6	1.9	0.2	9.5
Malaysia	—	—	—	—	—	—	3.8	0.7	5.4	1.2	0.2	6.0	—	—	—	—	—	—
Philippines	23.6	4.2	5.6	18.7	3.8	4.9	—	—	—	—	—	—	—	—	—	—	—	—
Viet Nam	—	—	—	—	—	—	—	—	—	—	—	—	10.0	1.7	5.9	4.7	0.8	5.9
Afghanistan	5.7	0.3	19.0	0.3	0.3	1.0	—	—	—	—	—	—	—	—	—	—	—	—
Bangladesh	—	—	—	—	—	—	7.6	6.4	1.2	1.7	—	—	—	—	—	—	—	—
India	6.3	0.5	12.6	1.6	—	—	10.8	1.5	7.2	4.1	0.2	20.5	—	—	—	—	—	—
Nepal	—	—	—	—	—	—	7.9	0.5	15.8	2.1	—	—	—	—	—	—	—	—
Pakistan	—	—	—	—	—	—	7.5	0.8	9.4	2.5	0.1	25.0	—	—	—	—	—	—
Sri Lanka	2.4	0.6	4.0	1.1	0.2	5.5	—	—	—	—	—	—	—	—	—	—	—	—
Solomon Islands	—	—	—	—	—	—	11.1	2.7	4.1	8.7	1.1	7.9	—	—	—	—	—	—

— Data not available.
U = Urban population; R = Rural population; U/R = Urban/Rural ratio.
Note: Data refer to population 25 years old and over.

Source: ADB 1993, 161-6.

completion ratio was as high as 45.9 times in Pakistan and 15.6 times in Nepal. It is not surprising that the urban-rural gap is even wider in tertiary enrollments. In India and Pakistan, the tertiary enrollment rates of females in urban areas were respectively 20.5 and 25.0 times those of females in rural areas (Table 25).

Looking at India specifically, illiteracy in rural areas exceeds that in urban areas, but the pattern is reversed in enrollments. Moreover, females accounted for 80.1 percent of rural illiteracy, whereas the corresponding proportion of male illiteracy was just about half in 1981. Referring to education enrollments, it is also clear that the higher the level of education, the wider the gap between urban and rural areas. In terms of male enrollments, the urban/rural ratio was 1.2 at the secondary level. It rose to 3.2 at the matriculation level, and further to 3.8 at the diploma level. The urban-rural gap was even wider among females. The urban/rural ratio was 2.2 at the secondary level. It rose to 7.4 at the matriculation level, but dropped slightly to 5.0 at the diploma level. Despite a small decrease in the urban-rural gap, the gap among females was still obviously wider than that among males at the diploma level (Table 26).

Nevertheless, in some countries urban-rural differences in education access are minimal. For example, enrollment rates are close to equal between urban and rural areas at a ratio of 1.1:1 in the Philippines and Sri Lanka across age groups, 1.1:1 in Viet Nam at the primary level, and 1.2:1 in Cambodia at the literacy level. In the Philippines, however, survival rates are higher in urban areas than in rural areas at an urban/rural ratio of 1.4:1. Moreover, the urban poor have slightly better education opportunities than the rural poor (Balisacan 1996, 526). The Republic of Korea has achieved parity between urban and rural enrollments, but this only applies to the school level. The urban-rural gap emerges in tertiary enrollments at a ratio of 2.4:1 (Table 27).

Regional differences in enrollments are also more obvious among females at higher levels of education. Inequality in access to education is not only higher in rural than urban regions, but also seems to have increased over time (Gertler and Rahman 1994, 155-6; Jayaweera 1991, Appendix 1, 2; Maitra, 1985; McDonald 1995, 26).

It is interesting to note that the Philippines, in respect to higher education female enrollments, has a far higher proportion of enrollments from rural

Table 26: Education Level of Population by Residence in India, 1981

Level of education	Male			Female		
	U%	R%	U/R	U%	R%	U/R
Illiterate	34.2	59.2	0.6	52.2	80.1	0.6
High school	42.4	34.5	1.2	35.6	16.5	2.2
Matriculation level	16.9	5.3	3.2	9.3	1.3	7.4
Diploma	0.7	0.2	3.8	0.2	0.04	5.0

U = Urban population; R = Rural population; U/R = Urban/Rural ratio.

Source: United Nations 1995, 29.

Table 27: Student Enrollment Rate by Education Level and Region in the Republic of Korea, 1985

Level of education	Urban (%)	Rural (%)	Urban/Rural
Primary school	100.6	104.4	1.0
Middle school	98.6	99.8	1.0
High school	89.7	80.0	1.1
University/College	44.9	18.6	2.4

Source: Chung and Oh 1994, 326.

backgrounds in most regions. Table 28 shows that the rural/urban ratio could be as high as 7 in Region X, but that Regions III and V and the National Capital Region (NCR) were approaching equality. The better universities are situated

Table 28: Percentage of Female Students from Urban and Rural Backgrounds by Region in the Philippines, 1970s and 1980s

Region	1975/76			1980/81			1985/86		
	U%	*R%*	*U/R*	*U%*	*R%*	*U/R*	*U%*	*R%*	*U/R*
Region I	15.0	46.5	0.32	14.9	41.6	0.36	17.5	38.3	0.46
Region II	18.2	40.5	0.45	19.0	44.7	0.43	19.8	45.1	0.44
Region III	28.1	27.5	1.02	29.4	29.1	1.01	35.4	30.2	1.17
Region IV	23.6	43.8	0.54	27.2	39.7	0.69	26.0	41.8	0.62
Region V	32.0	28.0	1.14	32.8	56.9	0.58	31.3	31.0	1.01
Region VI	23.7	39.5	0.60	26.3	38.9	0.68	24.0	38.3	0.63
Region VII	18.7	31.4	0.60	21.8	34.6	0.63	22.3	35.5	0.63
Region VIII	10.4	54.7	0.19	11.3	52.3	0.22	10.2	50.9	0.20
Region IX	14.7	40.9	0.36	21.5	32.5	0.66	23.3	33.8	0.69
Region X	6.8	52.8	0.13	7.1	50.2	0.14	9.1	48.9	0.19
Region XI	17.2	52.9	0.33	18.0	53.5	0.34	18.7	51.6	0.36
Region XII	21.5	45.9	0.47	20.8	43.3	0.48	20.0	45.9	0.44
National Capital Region	27.9	28.4	0.98	27.4	34.5	0.79	31.5	29.9	1.05

U = Urban population; R = Rural population; U/R = Urban/Rural ratio.

Source: Based on data from Mendez 1990, 127-8.

Box 6: "Education is Useless": Pressure for Rural Schooling in the PRC

In the PRC, the costs of rural schooling began to climb as the advantage of nonattendance rose under the new household responsibility system. Peasant families were given more incentives and more opportunities to make money in the 1980s. Their economic well-being suddenly depended on using their children to provide working hands on private family land.

One result was the appearance of available youth waiting to be engaged in lucrative occupations. In order to become rich, the youth farmed the land, were employed by the newly flourishing rural factories, or learned particular skills. The desire of each family for instant wealth was reflected in a prevailing attitude that education was useless, tasteless, and profitless, especially when peasant parents saw how much and how quickly money could be earned by a family business. Education was seen as a waste of time and money compared with the benefits of early employment.

As the rural reform gathered strength, household-run industries flourished in rural areas. Low-paid child labor became very common in many suburban and rural areas during the 1980s. Rural factory managers were eager to employ school dropouts and other youths.

Moreover, the closure of many rural schools made it difficult for children to pursue an education. Closures increased the distance between schools and homes; and instead of spending money on bus fares or boarding, many rural children moved into the suburbs or cities. Girls commonly found employment as domestic servants, and boys worked in newly expanded enterprises.

Source: Yang 1992, 101.

in the NCR. In 1975/76 and 1980/81, the urban/rural ratios among females were 0.98 and 0.79 respectively, but rose to 1.05 in 1985/86. This was probably a result of both the Government's deconcentration policy and the increased cost of staying in Metropolitan Manila (Mendez 1990, 128).

Regional Disparity within Countries

Beyond the urban-rural division, particularly in large countries, are other types of regional disparities. These disparities can be based on geographic location, for example the hills versus Terai of Nepal, the coastal versus inland regions in the PRC, and the lowlands versus uplands in the Lao PDR. In Nepal, the Central Development Region has the highest concentration of university graduates, with one graduate per every 102 population. The graduate/ population ratios in the other regions are much lower: 1:261 in the Eastern Development Region, 1:563 in the Mid-Western Development Region, and 1:542 in the Far Western Development Region (Bajracharya, Thapa, and Chitrakar 1997, 21). In respect of female enrollments, the Central Development Region alone has one fifth of the total higher education places in the country, leaving the other regions with very low proportions of higher education enrollments. In the peripheral regions such as the Mid-Western and Far Western Development Regions, almost no females enter tertiary institutions and in 1985 their enrollments accounted for only 5.8 percent and 2.7 percent, respectively, in secondary schools (Shrestha, Pradhan, Ghimier, and Singh 1990, 87). Moreover, as shown in Table 29, the hill region far exceeds the Terai in all sorts of higher education.

In India, women's share of earned income in Kerala is only 12 percent, while their share in Himachal Pradesh is 38 percent, and in Maharashtra 30 percent. In Andhra Pradesh, Madhya Pradesh, Gujarat, and Karnataka, their shares are over 25 percent. Yet Kerala ranks highly in education terms because the disparity between its female and male adult literacy rates is the lowest among the 16 states. The female literacy rate in Kerala is 81 percent, only 11 percentage points lower than that for males. Orissa, Madhya Pradesh, Rajasthan, Bihar, and Uttar Pradesh have GDI values so low that they can be compared only with impoverished countries such as Haiti, Nepal, and Yemen (UNDP 1996, 34).

Table 29: Female Enrollments in Higher Education by Geographic Region in Nepal, 1980 and 1985
(frequency)

| | 1980 | | | | 1985 | | | |
| | Certificate | Post-graduate | | | Certificate | Post-graduate | | |
Region		Bachelor		Total		Bachelor		Total
Hills	4,834	1,101	388	6,223	9,641	1,917	609	12,167
Terai	318	—	—	318	449	13	—	462

— Data not available.

Source: Shrestha, Pradhan, Ghimier, and Singh 1990, 74.

In Indonesia, as shown in Figure 3, regional differences in Gini coefficients continue to exist. Although some provinces show improvement in income equality, others have worsened. Moreover, as shown in Figure 4, regional differences persist despite a general decline in illiteracy across regions. School enrollment rates in the age group of 7-12 exceed 90 percent in almost all provinces. Java and Bali are well above the average primary graduate rate of 68 percent, while all of the eastern islands are below or near the average. The lowest completion rates are in East Nusa Tenggara, and Irian Jaya. Likewise, Sumatra and Jakarta have significantly less illiteracy than the national average, along with parts of Kalimantan and Sulawesi. Illiteracy rates are highest in West Nusa Tenggara and Irian Jaya. Bali and parts of Java continue to have higher than average illiteracy, which is consistent with the still-high numbers of the poor in these regions (World Bank 1996b, 115). This seems to correlate with regional disparities in terms of income poverty. In 1993, the incidence

Figure 3: Provincial Gini Coefficients in Indonesia, 1984 and 1993

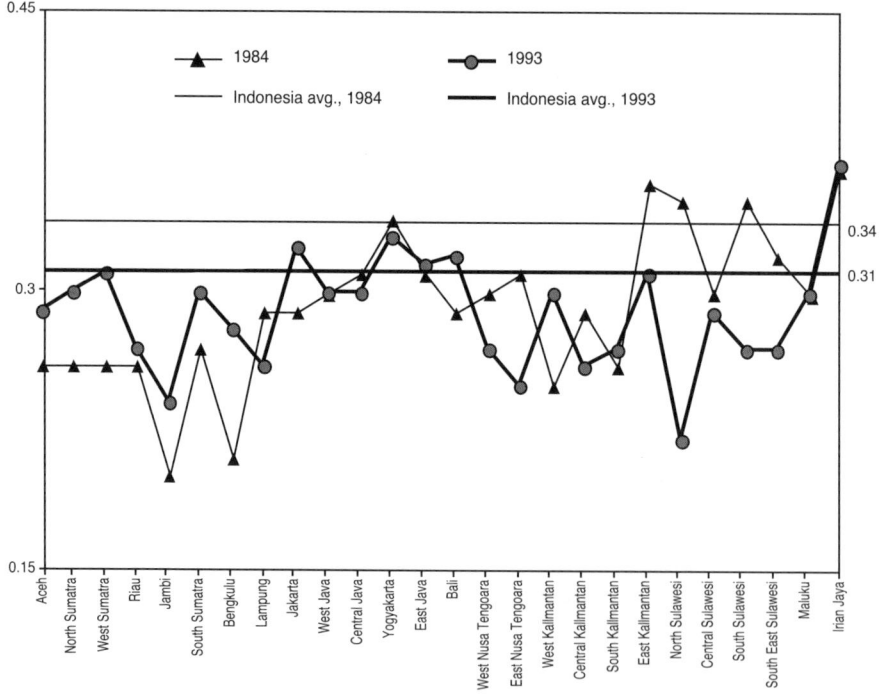

Notes: Estimates for Maluku and Irian Jaya were the same in 1983 and 1993.
No data are available for East Timor.

Source: World Bank 1996b, 99.

Figure 4: Provincial Illiteracy in Indonesia, 1980 and 1990

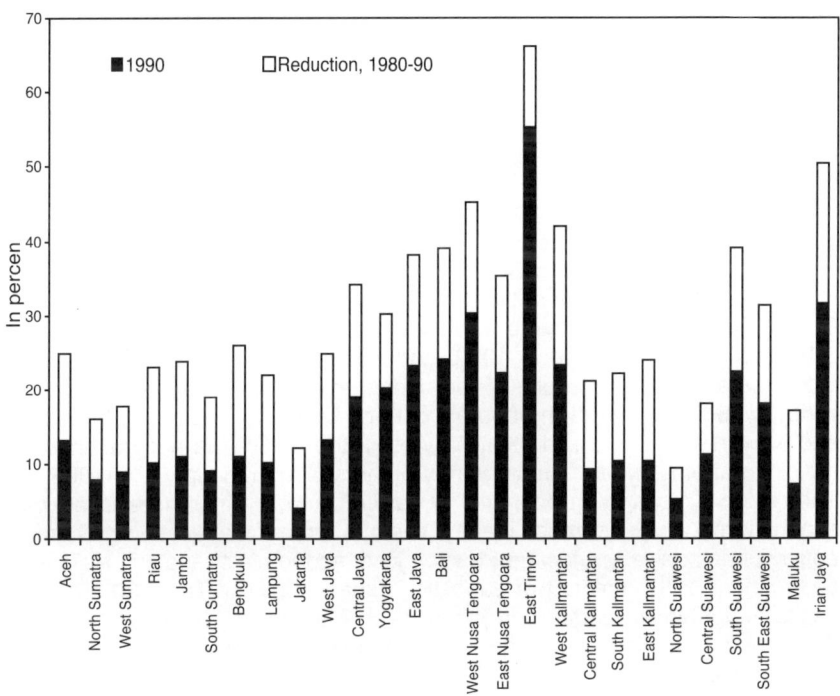

Note: Data for East Timor refer to 1985.

Source: World Bank 1996b, 115.

of income poverty was less than 10 percent in Jakarta, Yogyakarta, and Bali, but over 40 percent in East Nusa Tenggara, Iran Jaya, and West Kalimantan. Such disparities are also observed in the regional human development indices (UNDP 1997, 43).

Reasons for Regional Disparities: The Case of the PRC

The case of the PRC is illustrative for exploring the issue of regional disparities. The PRC is one of the four countries in the world, together with Brazil, Nigeria, and Egypt, with the greatest regional disparities. The PRC has a regional disparity coefficient much wider than that of India.

Table 30: Per Capita Budgeted Expenditure in Primary Schools in Selected Provinces in the PRC, 1988-1990
(yuan)

Province	1988	1989	1990
Beijing	217.8	246.0	289.7
Zhejiang	102.8	119.9	132.0
Shanxi	74.1	78.8	92.4
Shandong	58.7	68.3	77.1
Hubei	45.1	46.4	61.5
National Average	77.4	90.9	105.4

Source: Cheng 1995, 59.

The relative GDP per capita disparity between the richest and the poorest regions also began to widen: GDP per capita of Shanghai was 7.3 times that of Guizhou in 1990, and grew to 9.9 times in 1994. Similarly, Guangdong's was 3.1 times that of Guizhou in 1990, and it rose to four times in 1993. As an extreme case, the per capita of the richest town Zhuhai (a special economic zone) is 86 times that of the poorest county, Qinglong in Guizhou (Hu, Wang, and Kang 1995, 60-61). In most provinces, the per capita national income in the city proper is two to four times that of the suburban county (Cui 1995, 251). The regional disparity in economy is easily linked to differences in education expenditure, which is most clearly seen in primary education. As primary education is basically a local endeavor, local economic strength is a significant determinant of the amount of education expenditure. As Table 30 shows, per capita budgeted expenditure in primary schools is much higher in Beijing and Zhejiang than in Shandong and Hebei, and Beijing's expenditure is 4.7 times that of Hubei.

A number of factors contribute to the regional differences. The introduction of the open door policy has led to the establishment of special economic zones and opening up of the coastal regions. These zones and open regions have been given more autonomy for experimenting with the free market economy. As a result, the share of industrial output of the eastern coastal regions in the total increased from 59 percent in 1978 to 64 percent in 1991, whereas the share of the western regions declined from 14 percent to 12 percent (Yeh 1995, 179). Moreover, human poverty is far more pervasive in the remote interior provinces of the west (with an HPI of 44 percent) than on the coast (with an HPI of 18 percent) (UNDP 1997, 23). The average income of the farmers in the eastern regions is also notably higher: in 1980, it was Y217 in the eastern regions and Y181 in the central regions; in 1995, the respective incomes were Y2,127 and Y1,403. Whereas a farmer's income in the eastern regions was 1.2 times that in the central regions in 1980, it grew to 1.5 times in 1995 (Sun and Liang 1997, 107). Another factor was the region's proximity to the political center, which has become another attraction for foreign investments. The result is that the remote areas suffer. In 1990, Shanghai and Beijing attracted foreign investment of $177 million and $106 million, comparable to that of the open economic zones such as Guangzhou ($117 million) and Shenzhen ($349 million). The outlying regions have become explicitly disadvantaged, for example $30 million in Qingdao and $27 million in Shenyang, although both are classified as extra-large cities in the PRC (Sun and Liang 1997, 174).

A phenomenon related to regional development is the emergence of a large floating population in the regions with fast economic growth. In the mid-1990s, the floating population was about 80 million, and it was estimated that 120 million more would leave rural regions for work in the cities (UNDP 1996, 94). The brain drain toward the cities has increased pressure on developments in the rural regions.

In terms of education access and equity, causes of regional differences vary. One factor is a matter of 'center and periphery'. For example, because of their historical significance as political and cultural centers, Beijing, Shanghai, and Tianjin have become centers for education provision, and have therefore created a concentration of higher institutions. Concomitant with this is their enjoyment of a quite highly qualified population. For example, per 10,000 population in the late 1980s and early 1990s, there were approximately 190 tertiary students in Shanghai, 160 in Beijing, and 70 in Tianjin, versus a national figure of 23. Moreover, Beijing, Tianjin and Liaoning possess 24 percent of the natural sciences specialists, and 31 percent of the research and development personnel of the country (Hook and Lee 1998, 152). This implies that the regions distant from the political centers are more deprived in education provision.

Another factor for regional disparity relates to the pace of economic development in different regions. Regions that are better developed economically may also achieve a higher proportion of educated population. As Table 31 shows, Guangzhou, capital of Guangdong Province, achieved a ratio of 546 higher education graduates per 10,000 population in 1990, and Shenzhen, a special economic zone, achieved a ratio of 447. They were very close to Shanghai's ratio of 653, quite far from Beijing's 930, but well above the national ratio of 142 and the Guangdong provincial ratio of 134.

Box 7: Regional Disparity in Education in the PRC

The PRC has major disparities in education opportunities, resources, school facilities, teacher qualifications, and school achievements. Factors in these disparities include the government policy of differential regional development. Egalitarian principles may not be easily carried out in the face of other needs of the country, such as developing keypoint schools. The idea of keypoint schools is hardly egalitarian, in the sense of deliberately concentrating the best facilities and teachers in a few schools. The policy has been criticized since its implementation, but is considered necessary by the Government to speed up national development.

City population control is another conspicuous factor leading to the bright students of the fringe areas being deprived of opportunities to study in the best urban schools. Further, the differences in average annual income of workers in the cities and counties, as a result of rapid economic development, lead to education inequalities based on families' socioeconomic backgrounds.

Source: Lee and Li 1995, 73.

Table 31: Education Attainment of Selected Regions in the PRC, 1990
(per 10,000 population)

Region	Higher education graduates	Secondary graduates
Guangdong	134	3,197
Pearl River Delta	267	4,037
Guangzhou	546	4,378
Shenzhen	447	6,275
Zhuhai	256	4,436
Five other cities of Pearl River Delta	91	3,577
Beijing	930	4,953
Shanghai	653	5,122
PRC (as a whole)	142	3,138

Source: Liu, Wong, Sung, and Lau 1992, 88.

Table 32: Urban/Rural Ratio in Primary and Secondary Enrollments in the PRC, 1994

Primary	Urban/ Rural rate	Junior secondary	Urban/ Rural rate	Senior secondary	Urban/ Rural rate
1	0.16	1	0.29	1	2.01
2	0.16	2	0.29	2	2.10
3	0.16	3	0.32	3	2.02
4	0.17	4	0.39		
5	0.19				
6	0.31				
Total	0.18		0.30		2.04

Source: Adapted from *China Education Statistical Yearbook* 1994, 56-7, 78-9.

Ignoring the present semi-urban areas (i.e., townships), enrollments in cities versus rural areas provides a quick insight into educational access in the PRC. At the primary level, the rural-urban gap in enrollment rates has narrowed considerably, such that the headcount ratio of urban to rural pupils (see Table 32) more closely reflects the relative population shares of children in the appropriate age range. However, a sharply contrasting pattern appears at higher levels of schooling. By the senior secondary (noncompulsory) level, total urban enrollments are more than double those in rural areas. Nearly all provinces and municipalities achieve primary enrollments above 96 percent, the exceptions being the two remote and very poor provinces, Tibet (52.4 percent) and Qinghai (83.9 percent). Moreover, the remote and poor regions have significantly higher dropout rates, with the highest in Guizhou (8.0 percent) and Tibet (7.0 percent), compared with 0.9 percent in Zhejiang. At the secondary level, figures are 15.0 percent in Qinghai, 14.4 percent in Gansu, 13.9 percent in Ningxia, and 10.3 percent in Tibet. These figures compare with the national average of 4.7 percent. A similar picture can also be found in repetition rates (Wu 1995, 81, 82, 100).

A third factor relates to regional histories. For example, within Guangzhou (Canton), the historical significance of the central region has become the root for different education provisions compared with the large city region. Despite provincial government efforts to alleviate regional differences, there is a high demand for education in the central region, and a reluctance for people to move to other regions or to send their children elsewhere for education. In 1989, the average annual per capita education expenditure in primary and secondary schools was Y1,053.5 in the central region, compared with Y796 in the newly developed cities and Y397 in the counties (Lee and Li 1995, 72).

Reports from other DMCs suggest a similar picture. An ADB report on human development in the Lao PDR (1996b, 22) points out that inequities in education are higher in remote, mountainous, and plateau areas than in low-land areas. Gender disparities are also greater among the Midland Lao and the Upland Lao communities than among the Lowland Lao communities. The disparity is larger in poorer communities where living conditions are harsh. These patterns are reflected in sharp urban-rural disparities in per capita education subsidies.

The pressure on rural and female enrollments caused by migration is also found in other Asian countries. Referring to the case of India, Todaro (1997) points out that individuals with higher levels of education will face wider urban-rural real income differentials and higher probabilities of obtaining modern sector jobs than those with lower levels of education. Hence it is more likely for educated rural migrants to go to urban areas, for better employment and personal development. This explains the high percentage of illiterates in rural areas, the majority of whom are females. Hence it is expected that the migration rate for males – who are more readily able to secure an education – to urban areas is much higher than that for females. Similar scenarios can also be found in Fiji Islands, Papua New Guinea, Solomon Islands, and Vanuatu, where rural to urban migration is mainly a male movement, leaving women to maintain both the family and subsistence production (ADB 1996d, 23).

Urban Poverty

Despite general deprivation in rural areas, opportunities in urban areas are not necessarily better. In South Asia in 1990, while 47 percent of the rural populace

Table 33: Gini Index in Rural and Urban Areas in Selected DMCs, 1970s and 1980s
(percent)

Country	Circa 1976		Circa 1980		Circa 1984		Circa 1986	
	Urban	Rural	Urban	Rural	Urban	Rural	Urban	Rural
Bangladesh[a]	51	44	42	36	35	35	36	37
Indonesia[b]	36	31	36	31	32	28	32	26
Korea, Republic of[c]	42	33	41	36	37	30	35	29
Philippines[d]	44	45	—	—	44	38	43	38
Sri Lanka[e]	51	49	44	42	62	56	—	—

— Data not available.
[a] Data refer to 1981, instead of 1980.
[b] Data refer to 1987, instead of 1986.
[c] Data refer to 1985, instead of 1984; 1988, instead of 1986.
[d] Data refer to 1971, instead of 1976; 1985, instead of 1984; 1988, instead of 1986.
[e] Data refer to 1978, instead of 1976; 1985, instead of 1984.

Sources: Chang 1991, 6; Quibria 1994, 84, 399; Quibria 1996, 97, 436.

Box 8: Access and Equity in Education in the Philippines

Overall access to education in the Philippines is biased toward learners in the NCR and in relatively developed regions in Luzon, the Visayas, and Mindanao; and to relatively urbanized and affluent communities within each region. Middle- and upper-class children have greater access to education than children of poor families. Participation rates of the school-aged groups at each level of formal education have consistently increased over the years, reaching an average of 95 percent, 60 percent, and 30 percent of the total school age populations for elementary, secondary, and tertiary education, respectively, at the turn of the 1990s. However, these participation rates varied across regions, with lower rates in less developed regions and relatively depressed communities within each region.

Access to better equipped schools and adequate learning resources was more likely in economically advantaged regions, private sectarian schools in urban communities, and for children of upper-class families. Disparities in access between developed and less developed regions, urban and rural communities, and rich and poor children were exacerbated by policies and practices within the education system, indicated by the following conditions:

- incomplete primary and/or elementary schools in depressed and geo-graphically isolated communities;
- predominance of underqualified teachers and personnel in depressed communities;
- concentration of post-secondary education programs in the NCR and urban communities;
- concentration of tertiary institutions and access to tertiary level programs in Luzon, especially in the NCR;
- inequitable and uneven dispersal of nonformal education programs in the country;
- limited access to education opportunities among minorities;
- special education programs for gifted children, and for physically and mentally handicapped children, concentrated in the NCR and scarcely available in other regions; and
- limited and unequal access to early childhood programs of children in rural and depressed communities.

Source: Philippines 1997, 185-6.

lived in income poverty, the urban populace living in income poverty also accounted for 36 percent (UNDP 1997, 42). Table 33 shows that Gini indices are higher in urban areas than in rural areas, across countries and time, despite the state of economy or whether income inequalities within the country are widening or narrowing.

The Republic of Korea has achieved improvements in rural wage levels, and the disparity between the urban and rural areas has been reduced. According to a 1989 household survey, the average income of a rural farmer household was 103 percent of the average urban employee household, compared with 75.6 percent in 1970; the improvement in rural economic conditions was clearly enormous. However, associated with this was a problem of urban poverty. Gini coefficients in urban areas dropped from 0.39 in 1980 to 0.34 in 1989, and in rural areas from 0.35 to 0.29, so although both urban and rural Gini coefficients declined, urban income inequality continued to be wider than that of rural areas. Studies in the Republic of Korea projected that absolute poverty would continue to decrease, but that the problem of relative poverty would become more serious (Chang 1991, 4, 6, 9).

Statistics from Indonesia show that unemployment rates are higher in urban areas than in rural areas across education levels and genders. In the early 1980s, the average urban unemployment rate was 2.9 percent for males and 3.5 percent for females; and the rural unemployment rate was 1.1 percent for males and 2.1 percent for females (Daroesman 1985, 179). Urban unemployment was clearly more acute than rural unemployment, and females' unemployment rates were higher than males' in both urban and rural areas. However, the urban-rural difference among the females was less obvious than that among the males. The private components of primary school costs are two to three times higher in urban schools than in rural schools. Moreover, the costs in urban schools in Jakarta are 6.5 times higher than the national urban average while the costs in rural schools in Jakarta are 3.9 times higher than the national rural average (Table 34). This suggests that the living and education expenses are higher in urban areas, and so is the risk of unemployment. In Viet Nam, urban fees are higher than rural ones; and the fees increase steadily through the grades. In 1993, urban charges were between 1.2 and 1.5 times those of rural areas (Table 35).

Table 34: Percentage of Private Components of Primary School Costs in Indonesia, 1989
(percent)

	Public schools	Private schools	Urban schools	Rural schools	Urban/ Rural	Total
Jakarta	29.0	91.9	88.2	26.6	3.3	39.0
Other Java	9.3	48.7	30.2	8.6	3.5	10.0
Outside Java	3.5	12.6	8.5	3.5	2.4	4.2
Indonesia (as a whole)	7.8	30.0	13.4	6.8	2.0	8.8

Source: Bray 1996, 36.

Table 35: Official Fees for Grades 6-12 in Viet Nam, 1993
(dong per student)

Grade	Per month		Per year[a]		Urban/ Rural
	Urban	Rural	Urban	Rural	
6	3,000	2,000	27,000	18,000	1.50
7	4,000	3,000	36,000	27,000	1.33
8	5,000	4,000	45,000	36,000	1.25
9	6,000	5,000	54,000	45,000	1.20
10	7,000	5,000	63,000	45,000	1.40
11	8,000	6,000	72,000	54,000	1.33
12	9,000	7,000	81,000	63,000	1.29

[a] Monthly fees are paid for a nine-month school year.

Source: Bray 1996, 17.

Policy Implications

Regional disparities exist everywhere, and there is no simple remedy for them. Sometimes, attempted remedies cause other problems. For example, regions identified as disadvantaged may wish to maintain this identity to retain eligibility for preferential policies such as tax reductions, special subsidies, and student quotas. Even centrally planned economies have been unable to eliminate regional disparities, while liberalization of economies has generally enlarged disparities. Many factors are of course involved, but the focus of discussion here is confined to relationships between disparities and education.

In the PRC, the complexity of regional disparities in education is not confined to distribution of resources. Although national higher institutions are concentrated in major cities, residents of these cities complain about their relative disadvantage in entering the national key universities because special quotas are given to the disadvantaged regions. However, the disadvantaged regions do not necessary "gain" from these quotas, as sending the top students to the national key universities may contribute to a brain drain. For example, Hayhoe (1995, 85-6) reports that Hubei and Hunan respectively send about 8,000 and 10,000 of their best students to national universities every year. The brain drain poses a formidable problem for these regions.

Focusing on education, many of the issues and policy implications are common to those in the previous section, i.e., special help given to the poor. Additional policy considerations in relation to those discussed in this section include:

(i) *Enhancing relevance and improving the quality of schooling.* This is particularly important for rural areas, as a major cause for school nonattendance, apart from school factors, is that parents and children do not see the relevance of schooling to their daily lives, work, and job opportunities. A successful experience in a poor rural region, the County of Conghua in Guangzhou, is to emphasize vocational and technical education, and provide the type of skill training that is relevant to the needs of the region. Moreover, the local government encourages the schools to establish close relationships with urban keypoint schools, asking them to send good teachers and provide training to local teachers and administrators, as a means of enhancing the quality of schooling. As a result, their lower secondary enrollment rate rose from 62.6 percent in 1986 to 95.0 percent in 1988 (Lee and Li 1995, 77).

(ii) *Building partnerships and mobilizing local resources.* Part of the solution to regional disparities in education is collaboration between central and local governments to solve the problems of local schooling. Bangladesh is testing an approach for developing community schools, in which the Government pays construction costs and contributes to the teacher's salary, whereas the community provides the land and assumes overall responsibility for the school's operating expenses. In Pakistan, Education Foundations have been established in every province and at the national level. Such foundations raise 50 percent of the cost of opening a new school from the private sector, an NGO, or a community organization.

(iii) *Improving efficiency in distribution of aid across regions.* As noted, government subsidies can benefit the nonpoor more than the poor if governments are not careful in the mechanisms of distribution of subsidies. External aid can easily fall into the same trap. According to an ADB study of human development in Cambodia (1996a, 84), despite greater need for aid in the disadvantaged areas, education assistance has been disproportionately directed to the more developed areas of the country. The per capita aid received in Phnom Penh can be many times higher than that in the other regions (Figure 5). This means that while needy groups have no or very little access to aid, there may be problems of management and delivery of aid in the regions where aid is concentrated. Governments need to pay special attention to divert aid to the more needy regions.

Figure 5: NGO Education/Training Assistance, per Capita, by Province in Cambodia, 1995

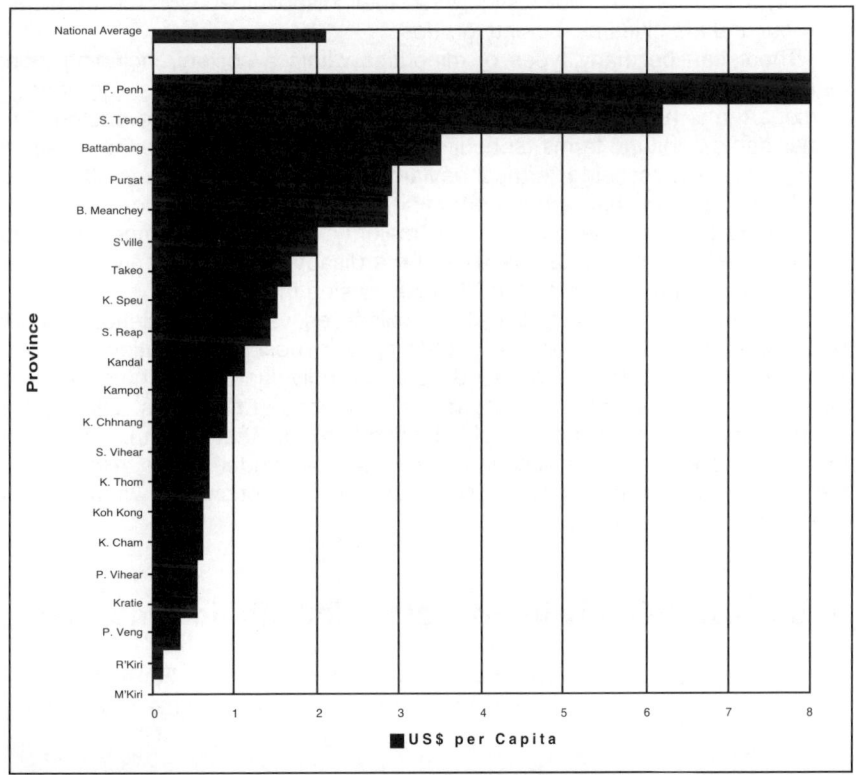

Source: ADB 1996a, 84.

Sociocultural-Related Equity

Institutional and sociocultural issues have major implications for project success and/or failure. School attendance and life chances for the disadvantaged are strongly affected by sociocultural perceptions. For example, the school attendance of females may be hindered by sociocultural perceptions that, should a choice have to be made, boys should receive priority in going to school. This is most clear in tertiary enrollments since education at this level demands more private financial contributions, and in rural enrollments where girls are seen as ready laborers. The disadvantage of rural residents is also affected by the relevance of education to their living, particularly when investment in education has significant opportunity costs.

This section looks at education opportunities for a disadvantaged group not covered in the last three sections on gender-related, income-related, and region-related equity. They are the minorities within various societies. Their disadvantages can be closely related to, or even a combination of, the above three types of inequity; but distinctively, their disadvantages come from their sociocultural identities as minority groups.

There can be many types of minorities within a society, including those defined in economic terms (the income poor); political terms (dissidents); religious terms (those not affiliating to the state religion could be another kind of dissidents); cultural terms (subcultural groups, dissidents from the dominant culture, sometimes being termed deviants/delinquents); language (those not speaking the national language); and ethnicity (the ethnic minorities). Sometimes the minorities can be the "majority" in terms of number (e.g., the income poor). In this sense, there can be a disadvantaged majority as well as an advantaged minority (e.g., the Chinese outside the PRC).

Data on minorities are difficult to collect, as very few societies officially collect data according to the above definitions, especially in relation to access and equity in education. It is also difficult for individual researchers to mount large-scale surveys that represent the various types of minorities. This booklet will focus on one of the more easily identified groups, that is, ethnic minorities. In addition, the end of this section will link back to gender issues, especially in the context of examining how sociocultural perceptions of women have hindered their life chances.

Access and Equity in Education for Ethnic Minorities

Ethnic equity is a declared national policy for most countries. For example, the official aims of education in Singapore are expressed in terms of a tripartite policy of equality, unity, and relevance. By equality is meant equal treatment for the four major ethnic groups and their languages in society (Lee 1991, 58). Recent reform in Taipei, China particularly mentions an emphasis on vernacular education, acknowledging the significance of education for minorities, and granting recognition to the vernacular as a medium of instruction. However, study of ethnic minorities in DMCs on the one hand is limited by access to data, and on the other is complicated by the nature of minority issues. The major task of this part of the booklet is to report the situations of the ethnic minorities in various DMCs, based on the limited data available.

One complication in minority issues concerns the Chinese who are economically well-off but ethnically a small proportion in some countries. For example, in Malaysia, while the richest tenth of the population (most with Chinese background) increased their share of national income by 18 percent between 1957 and 1970, the poorest half (mostly Malays) saw their share fall by almost one third. By 1970 the per capita income of the Malays (54 percent of the population) was about half that of the non-Malays, and they accounted for only 25 percent of industrial employment. Economic and human development disparities between ethnic groups were seen as the root cause of the racial tensions which culminated in riots in 1969. After the riots, the Government took a two-pronged approach to translate rapid economic growth into human development for all. It adopted a 20-year perspective plan for promoting growth and human development, reducing poverty, and increasing equity. The Government has also made efforts to end racial discrimination in employment (UNDP 1996, 60).

In education, the Malays accounted for 72 percent of higher education enrollments in 1985/86. However, the non-Malays were also well represented in the major universities, e.g., 46 percent in the University of Malaya, 45 percent in the University of Science, and 28 percent in the National University of Malaysia. The high-achieving non-Malays, who are mostly Chinese, were able to gain entry to the key universities. The students at the other universities were mainly Malays, but largely those studying for certificate and diploma courses. For example, the Malays accounted for 93 percent of the student population in the International Islamic University and 81 percent in the Agricultural University of Malaysia (Selvaratnam 1987, 19). Likewise, while degree course enrollments were still dominated by the Malays in 1988 (62 percent), the Chinese fared well (31 percent). However, the certificate and diploma courses are mainly taken by the Malays (70 percent and 93 percent respectively) (Lee 1997, 190).

The above discussion is related to an "advantaged minority" group. Returning to the issue of disadvantaged minorities, data suggest that minorities within DMCs continue to be disadvantaged in access to education. This may be demonstrated by case studies of Cambodia, PRC, Lao PDR, and Nepal.

Case One: Cambodia

Nearly 90 percent of Cambodians are ethnic Khmers. The remaining 10 percent are diverse. They include Cham-Muslims, Vietnamese, Chinese,

Thais, Laotians, Filipinos, and members of hill tribes. The 200,000 Chinese have assimilated into Khmer society, and the 200,000 Cham-Muslims live in compact villages north and east of Phnom Penh, practicing their own religions. In addition, over 25 other groups, including Lao, Phnong, Kul, Tumpoun, and Koreung, are subsistence slash-and-burn farmers in the provinces of the north and east. Presently there are no coherent strategies for improving health, education, or training provision for ethnic minorities, mainly situated in the northern and northeastern provinces.

The minorities are vastly underrepresented in the mainstream provision of social services. Families suffer access constraints (such as distance to schools and clinics, and no money for books and drugs), which are characteristic of these provinces. Additional obstacles for minority children include language difficulties for non-Khmer speakers, lack of traditions of formal schooling and health care, and nomadic lifestyles (UNDP 1996, 16, 17).

Cambodia has other vulnerable groups, including 380,000 Cambodians who had been living in Thai border camps and who were later repatriated. The United Nations High Commissioner for Refugees estimates that one third of returning refugees remain vulnerable. They lack the security of family connections, and they lack links with local authorities. Ironically, many residents of the camps enjoy education opportunities not available to those who stayed in the country. There are classes in subjects ranging from English language to business administration. An estimated 3,000 camp residents have earned credentials as teachers and thousands more as medical technicians. Many returnees have experienced problems in finding work. Measures are needed to optimize this human resource base (UNDP 1996, 29).

Case Two: People's Republic of China

The PRC has 55 national minorities, totaling 80 million people, accounting for some 8 percent of the population, and occupying 62 percent of the country's total land area (or 90 percent of the country's border area), and cluster mainly in eight provinces and autonomous regions in the west: Inner Mongolia, Guangxi, Tibet, Ningxia, Xinjiang, Guizhou, Yunnan, and Qinghai. The minorities in the eight regions have much lower education attainments than the national average and the Han Chinese. In 1990, the national average for illiteracy and semi-illiteracy in the population aged 12 years and above was

Table 36: Education Attainments of National Minorities in the PRC, 1987
(per 10,000 population)

Level of education	Nationwide	Minorities	Nationwide/ Minorities
University	86	37	2.3
Upper secondary	682	455	1.5
Lower secondary	2,097	1,216	1.7
Primary	3,580	3,021	1.2

Source: Postiglione, Teng, and Ai 1995, 190.

16 percent. Five of the eight regions had a rate higher than the national average: Ningxia 23 percent, Guizhou 26 percent, Yunnan 27 percent, Qinghai 30 percent, and Tibet 49 percent. Illiteracy rates were particularly high among the minorities: 61 percent among Jinpo, Achang, and Ducong; 62 percent among Yi, Shui, and Sala; 63 percent among Nu; 69 percent among Luoba and Wa; 70 percent among Hani; 72 percent among Lisu; 73 percent among Daur; 76 percent among Baoan; 82 percent among Lahu; and 87 percent among Dongxiang. The minorities achieved a lower proportion of enrollments than the national average (Postiglione 1992, 308; Postiglione, Teng, and Ai 1995, 190-1). As shown in Table 36, apart from the primary level, in 1987 the proportion of enrollments among minorities fell short of the national average by about half.

Minority groups in the PRC generally live in areas where the soil is too poor for even subsistence crop production, so they are net buyers of food and have been hit hard by higher prices. The incidence of poverty in these groups is much higher than in the general population (UNDP 1997, 50). Primary schools in poor and minority areas often do not offer all six grades. About 30 percent of the rural primary schools in its project counties are incomplete schools, i.e., they do not offer the full primary program, and some offer only three or even fewer grades. Small villages are served by "teaching points," in which only two grades, 1 and 3, or 2 and 4, are offered. In 1993, their project counties had 9,726 such teaching points. Since complete primary schools may be located 4 to 5 kilometers away from small villages, and boarding schools are costly, many children discontinue their education after attending an incomplete school (World Bank 1996a, 5).

Case Three: Lao People's Democratic Republic

The Lao PDR is also characterized by strong ethnic and cultural diversity. The 1985 census identified 47 distinct ethno-linguistic groups. However, the main Laotian population can be grouped into three main ethnic groups, based on origins, history, and geographic locations of residence. The Lao Loum account for about 65 percent of the Laotian population. They reside in the stronger economic areas, i.e., the lowlands, and they play a dominant role in the country's political and economic system. The other two groups are the Lao Theung and Lao Soung, accounting for 20-25 percent and 10-15 percent of the population, respectively. Both these minority ethnic groups reside in the hilly uplands and practice swidden rice farming. They live in remote areas and have higher illiteracy, especially among women (65-80 percent). Dropout rates from primary education are exceedingly high (60-80 percent). These minorities also suffer from inadequate transport and lack of telecommunications networks (ADB 1996b, 3). As shown in Table 37, while the survival rates in education in the country are generally low, they are especially low among the Lao Theung and Lao Soung: whereas among the Lao Loum, out of 100 entrants to primary education only 32 and 13 completed lower and upper secondary education respectively, the respective figures among the Lao Theung were 11 and 1 and among the Lao Soung, 7 and 1.

Table 37: Survival Rates by School Type and Ethnic Group in the Lao PDR, 1991/92
(percent)

School type	Lao Loum	Lao Theung	Lao Soung	Total
Primary: New entrants	100	100	100	100
Primary: Graduates	56	25	26	39
Lower secondary: New entrants	43	15	15	36
Lower secondary: Graduates	32	11	7	21
Higher secondary: New entrants	19	3	3	15
Higher secondary: Graduates	13	1	1	8

Source: Netherlands Economic Institute 1995, 93.

Table 38: Literacy Rates by Ethnic Group in Nepal, 1997
(percent)

Ethnic group	Literacy rate	Ethnic group	Literacy rate
Dusadh	11	Sherpa	47
Chamar	11	Limbu	48
Dhobi	22	Gurung	48
Muslim	23	Thakuri	48
Tharu	28	Newar	61
Yadav	28	Thakali	63
Tamang	29	Brahmin	63
Magar	41	Kayastha	65
Rai	46	Marwari	88
Chetri	46		

Source: Bajracharya, Thapa, and Chitrakai 1997, 21.

Case Four: Nepal

Data from Nepal show great variations in literacy rates among the various ethnic groups. In 1997 the Dusadh and Chamar had a literacy rate of only 11 percent, whereas the Marwari had a literacy rate of 88 percent (Table 38). People in the disadvantaged groups (e.g., Rana Tharus) do not see education as relevant to improvement of their social and economic conditions. Moreover, the lack of confidence among people in these groups (e.g., Mushahar from Terai) poses a hindrance for them to participate in education.

The sociocultural barriers in Nepal are significant. As mentioned above, underachievement in education is commonly attributable to sociocultural perceptions on whether education is worthwhile. The low self-esteem of the minorities and the perceived socioeconomic irrelevance of education to them is certainly one factor for the minorities' underachievement in education. Another factor relates to subtle tensions among different ethnic groups, which is an issue much more difficult to resolve. Tan's (1993, 139-40) study of Chinese in the Philippines and Koreans in Japan has identified such a tension:

> Total assimilation of the Koreans has only been deterred by their not being accepted socially by the Japanese. The feeling of degradation has led many Koreans to hide their identity through the use of Japanese names....

For the Chinese in the Philippines, total assimilation is still being held back by the existence of the "three treasures" that the Chinese have in the community, i.e., the associations, the press, and the greatly "diluted" ex-Chinese schools.... [The] ethnic Chinese are different from other minorities because they have self-confidence while the other minorities lack self-esteem.

Gender Disparity from a Sociocultural Perspective

Gender disparity can also be viewed from a sociocultural perspective. As mentioned, despite general improvements in gender enrollments, females' access to education seems to be at best up to senior secondary attainment. Females tend to be barred from further development beyond that level of education, and the GEM is generally lower than the GDI across countries, especially in terms of opportunities for securing access to decision-making positions in employment. This means that females continue to be seen as the weaker sex in Asia, despite enhanced opportunities in recent years. Comments from various DMCs in respect to women's education opportunities and life chances all point to the sociocultural dimension.

(i) *East and Southeast Asia.* In East and Southeast Asia women's status seems to be improving, but substantial sociocultural barriers still exist. Filipino society, for example, holds an egalitarian norm in terms of equal work for equal pay for both genders, emphasizes the sovereignty of the family, and the responsibilities of motherhood. However, as far as education is concerned, sons are still seen as having priority over daughters if a choice has to be made (Mendez 1990, 144).

(ii) *Taipei,China.* Taipei,China has witnessed substantial improvements in females' education and occupation opportunities, and conspicuous waves of feminist movements in the last two decades. However, coming down to empowerment of women in society, it seems that there is still a long way to go. As Chou (1994, 352) notes:

> The phenomenon of the dominance of men in the employer class and women in the unpaid category persists over time. Similarly in occupational attainment, women's representation in the highest income-generating occupations (i.e., administrators and managers) is still very low and has remained so in the past two decades. In short, it may be said that while women may not have been excluded horizontally from the process of the emerging urban productive system, they have not been integrated vertically into the core of the production process either. Sex segregation at the level of ownership of the means of production remains the biggest obstacle in the way of gender equality.

(iii) *Hong Kong, China.* Likewise, in Hong Kong, China where females are relatively well represented in both education and employment, and where an Equal Opportunities Commission was established and a Sex Discrimination Ordinance was enacted in 1997, recent studies show substantial sociocultural perceptions that are disadvantageous to women. In education, analyses of textbooks show substantial sexual stereotyping. For example, in popular kindergarten textbooks, while fathers are usually described as wage-earners, mothers are described as housewives who stay at home and are responsible for household chores. Ma (1991) found only one mention of father doing household chores, but such mention was much clearer in regard to motherhood in the textbooks. Other studies of primary and secondary textbooks also show that men are depicted positively as heroes whereas women are pictured negatively as hindrances to men's success. Moreover, passive characteristics are mostly associated with women, such as docility, passivity, dullness, and lack of confidence (Yau and Luk 1990).

(iv) *The PRC.* Studies on women in the PRC commonly argue that the PRC is still influenced by a feudalistic view of women, advocating that virtuous women should be untalented, docile, and submissive (Shi 1995, 140). Referring to contemporary women's status in the PRC, Niu (1993, 26) notes that:

> The overall participation of females in Chinese education has increased since 1949, but significant disparities between men and women persist. Most of the participation of females is at the elementary level and low secondary level, while males continue to dominate the most important part of education – institutions of higher learning. Gender inequality is apparent not only in education, but also in other parts of the society. The gender inequality in Chinese society and the gender inequality in education influenced each other and made the situation of females worse... There appeared institutional discrimination in education and work, as well as promotion of social positions.... Female aspirations were usually low, which in return greatly prevented females from climbing up the social ladder.

(v) *Sri Lanka.* Women's status remains notably low in South Asia. Their conditions are far worse than their counterparts in East and Southeast Asia. Commenting on women in Sri Lanka, Jayaweera (1991, 9) argued that empowerment of women is simply difficult in a patriarchal society:

> Sociocultural factors that stem from patriarchal norms impinge strongly on the lives of women. The perceptions of policymakers, administrators, employers and in fact, of society, of men as breadwinners and women as dependent housewives or at most secondary earners, despite the reality of women's lives and their economic contribution, perpetuates the gender division in the labor market and the relative invisibility of women in development plans. Women are perceived to be passive consumers of services and are subsumed in

the family.... There is contradiction between patriarchal norms to which many women subscribe and the reality of women's centrality as mothers and as economic providers especially in low-income families. The acceptance by women of practices such as arranged marriages, the dowry system and domestic violence reflects the failure of education and economic participation to empower them to function as individuals with human rights and dignity.

(vi) *The Lao PDR.* ADB's report on human development in the Lao PDR (1996b, 23) comments that females' low attainment in education needs to be viewed in the larger context of Laotian society:

> Barriers to women's and girls' participation need to be viewed within the larger context of Laotian society. Cultural factors have shaped attitudes toward men and women. In poorer families, it's girls not boys who work at home instead of attending schooling, as a result of social attitudes that deem boys more worthy of education than girls.... The barriers to women's and girls' participation in education frequently described include: family maintenance, thus leaving little time for female participation in formal or nonformal education; family economics, which often dictate that given the limited resources boys are sent to school before girls because of the belief that boys have better opportunities for employment; perceived lack of benefits from education, both by rural families and women who may not link the benefits of education to their immediate lives leading to their disinterest in education programs.

(vii) *India.* Referring to women in India, the UNDP (1996, 34) simply says: "Women in India suffer on two counts – first, because the society as a whole is impoverished, and second, because they are women."

(viii) *Cambodia.* Similarly, ADB's report on human development in Cambodia (1996a, 28) notes that "Women are more likely than men to be among the poorest of the poor."

(ix) *Nepal.* It is striking to find a comment referring to modern Nepalese women that seems to portray a continued classical view of female inferiority:

> In many communities, women are treated as impure or as untouchable during their menstruation period, and in Jumla they are forced to spend this period outside their home. As one commentary puts it:

>> All the drudgeries of domestic life are to be shouldered by the women. She is the cook, the grinder, the water carrier, fuel or wood carrier, the washerwoman and utensil cleaner. On top of all that she is a cattle tender and a farm worker. All these would pass on as normal because she does them without a wail.

The lifestyle imposed on females is such that in most parts of rural Nepal, engagement in household chores is "naturally" expected of daughters, even at the expense of their schooling. Even those who are fortunate enough to start school often have to leave it abruptly, especially with the onset of puberty (Shrestha et al. 1990, 88).

In conclusion, the issue of gender-related equity is at heart a sociocultural issue. Measures should be taken not only to enhance education opportunities and economic participation, but also social and political participation of girls and women, and to change the social and cultural perception toward parity in gender status.

Policy Implications

Of the four aspects of equity, the sociocultural aspect is the most intractable. Sociocultural aspects of equity involve values, beliefs, and cultural traditions that are fundamental to the behavior of sociocultural groups and government policies. Although the review above has uncovered clear differences in education opportunities between cultural groups in terms of access, participation, and life chances, not all the minorities are bound to remain disadvantaged. For example, the Koreans are the most literate minority in the PRC, and the Chinese outside the PRC are generally an advantaged minority. It seems that the prospects for minorities are sometimes due to whether government policies are favorable to their development, but are sometimes also due to the determination and efforts of particular cultural groups. To facilitate identification of appropriate government policies, discussion here focuses on ways to tackle the problems with disadvantaged groups in general.

Changing Values, Beliefs, and Awareness

If values and beliefs are the fundamentals underlying the obstacles to achieving equity in education, becoming aware of the need to change values and beliefs toward equity is important for realizing the goal of equity. In this regard, a few concerns and principles may be emphasized:

(i) *Pluralistic society and cultural rights.* Most countries have multicultural populations, and awareness of cultural diversity and pluralism is fundamental to the improvement of the conditions of the ethnic/cultural minorities. Fundamental to the recent deregulation policies in Taipei, China that began to allow for education specifically oriented to aboriginal and vernacular education is awareness of the need for education for cultural diversity. The 1995 report of the Council on Educational Reform observes (p.58) that:

A society which is open and becoming democratic is bound to face the challenge of pluralism. In this regard, the aims of education should not only reflect pluralistic values and ideals; the contents of curriculum should also cater to the expectations of different cultural groups and cultural systems, and the education system should be adjusted to such a need.

This is consistent with the International Covenant on Economic, Social and Cultural Rights, which affirms the cultural right to education.

(ii) *Changing the values and beliefs of disadvantaged groups.* According to a 1993 study of the values of three ethnic groups in the PRC, the minorities are suffering from low self-esteem and low aspirations. Among the three ethnic groups – the Hans, Huis, and Zangs – respondents indicated that "ambitious," "broadminded," and "honest" were the most important values; but "capable" was rated most important only by the Hans, and "equality" only by the Zangs (Zhao, Chen, and Liu 1993). Likewise, many gender-related studies show that low self-esteem and aspirations of females can be an underlying cause for them not to push through with their education. Of course, the formation of such values or beliefs may be shaped by society at large. The need to change the general attitude to disadvantaged sociocultural groups is a challenge to the Government.

(iii) *Textbooks revised to avoid gender stereotyping.* One commonly identified aspect of education is the existence of gender stereotyping (and perhaps also cultural group stereotyping), which is a hidden cause for building unfavorable attitudes among and toward disadvantaged groups. Care is needed to rectify this element in textbooks.

Enhancing Equity and Access to Education

In addition to attending to the values and beliefs that may foster disadvantages, attention can be paid to the following aspects that can enhance equity and access for the disadvantaged:

(i) *Bilingual education.* A common problem facing minorities is that the language spoken in school is not the students' daily language. Chuard and Mingat (1996a, 19) in their dropout study have identified that in one case, 20 percent of Bhutanese pupils in Grade 4 were taught by a teacher who could not speak their language. This implies that having teachers who can speak their language and teach in the vernacular are important; but the complication is that the employment prospects of the minorities will be limited if they cannot master the national language, and some may even prefer learning the national language to their own vernacular (Mackerras 1995, 142-3). In this case, good monitoring of bilingual education is essential to allow preservation of culture and pedagogical efficiency, as well as the life chances of minorities.

(ii) *Training minority teachers.* Parallel to the need to facilitate self-help among the females and the poor is a need to facilitate self-help among minorities. In this context, training minority teachers to return to the minority areas is important. However, an obvious problem is again to avoid a brain drain, and the policy needs some reinforcement measures for the teachers to return to their homes to work with their people.

(iii) *Special assistance schemes and preferential policies for the needy.* As most minorities are income poor, special assistance schemes for the poor should also be applied to minorities. These include social support or welfare systems, regular home visits, free textbooks, boarding or tent schools, etc. (World Bank 1996a, 17).

Patterns of Access and Equity in Education by Country Groupings

The observations above mainly testify that despite economic growth and development, and despite generally enhanced education opportunities in DMCs, considerable inequities in access to education remain. In such a context it is worthwhile to identify ways in which DMCs differ from each other by country grouping. This section categorizes DMCs with reference to their HDI ranks, because access and equity is mainly an HDI issue. Groupings are also based on income levels (GNP per capita) and regional locations. As a result, DMCs are organized into three main groups:

Group L: This category includes countries classified by the *Human Development Report 1999* (UNDP 1999) as low in HDI (with an HDI value below 0.500) and low GNP per capita (below $765). They are mainly South Asian countries: Afghanistan, Bangladesh, Bhutan, Lao PDR, and Nepal. Their GNP per capita ranges between $200 and $400, positioned at the bottom of the low-income countries, compared with the ceiling of $765.

Group M: Countries in Group M fall in the medium range of HDI (between 0.500 and 0.799) and GNP per capita (between $765 and $9,385). In terms of geographic location, they are quite scattered. Twelve of these countries are in Southeast Asia and the Pacific (Cambodia, Fiji Islands, Indonesia, Malaysia, Myanmar, Papua New Guinea, Philippines, Samoa, Solomon Islands, Thailand, Vanuatu, and Viet Nam); the PRC and Mongolia; four in Central Asia (Kazakhstan, Kyrgyz Republic, Tajikistan, and Uzbekistan); and four in South Asia (India, Maldives, Pakistan, and Sri Lanka). Like Group L countries, nearly all the Group M countries are at the bottom of the medium range of GNP per capita. Seven of them should even belong to the low GNP per capita countries, but since the major guide for grouping is HDI, they are placed in this category.

Group H: The third category consists of the NIEs: Hong Kong, China; Republic of Korea; Singapore; and Taipei,China. They have high HDI (above 0.800) and high GNP per capita (above $9,385). However, due to unavailability of data, Taipei,China is not included in this analysis (Table 39).

Table 39: Classification of the Selected DMCs by HDI and Region, 1997

Country groupings by HDI and GNP per capita	Region	ADB developing member countries	HDI Rank[a]	GNP per capita ($)
Group L Low HDI and GNP per capita (HDI: below 0.5000; GNP per capita: below $765)	Mainly South Asia; except *	Bangladesh Bhutan Nepal Lao PDR* Afghanistan	150 145 144 140 —	360 430 220 400 —
Group M Medium HDI and GNP per capita (HDI: 0.5000–0.7999; GNP per capita: $765-$9,385)	Mainly Southeast Asia and the Pacific; except *	Pakistan* Cambodia India* Papua New Guinea Myanmar Mongolia* Solomon Islands Vanuatu Viet Nam Tajikistan* Indonesia PRC* Kyrgyz Republic* Maldives* Uzbekistan* Sri Lanka* Philippines Kazakhstan* Samoa Thailand Fiji Islands Malaysia	138 137 132 129 128 119 118 116 110 108 105 98 97 93 92 90 77 76 70 07 61 56	500 300 370 930 — 390 870 1,340 310 330 1,110 860 480 1,180 1,020 800 1,200 1,350 1,140 2,740 2,460 4,530
Group H High HDI and GNP per capita (HDI: 0.8000 and above; GNP per capita: above $9,385)	NIEs[b]	Korea, Republic of Hong Kong, China Singapore	30 24 22	10,550 25,200 32,810

— Data not available.

* = Countries that are not in the same region of the group.

[a] Table is sorted by this column heading.

[b] Data for Taipei,China are unavailable.

Sources: ADB 1999, 248; UNDP 1998, 225; 1999, 134-7, 180-3, 257.

Gender, Education Enrollments and Education Expenditure

Education Enrollment

According to Table 40, the GERs in the medium and high HDI countries are notably higher than those in the L countries. In terms of GERs, these countries have in general achieved universal primary education. However, the low HDI countries are still far from the target, with GERs only averaging 87.8 percent. The gap in GERs between the three groups of countries has become obvious starting from the secondary level of education onwards. The group H economies achieve an average secondary GER of 83.1 percent, whereas it is 55.2 percent for the M countries. This means that on average about half of the relevant age group in the medium GNP per capita countries have no access to secondary education. The average secondary GER in the L countries, i.e., mainly South Asian countries, is as low as 26.9 percent, implying that three quarters of the relevant age group have no access to secondary education. Tertiary education is obviously a privilege for a very small group of people in the L and M countries, with only 3.1 percent of GER in the former and 13.2 percent in the latter. At the higher education level, again, the H economies have a comparatively high average tertiary GER of 42.3 percent. The low GERs in the L countries is attributable to the exceptionally low figures in a few countries, namely 1.7 percent in Afghanistan and 0.2 percent in Bhutan. The relatively high tertiary GER in the group H economies may be attributed to an exceptionally high enrollment rate in the Republic of Korea, of which the tertiary GER is 60.3 percent (see Appendix 1, Table A1.9).

Public Current Expenditure on Higher Education

The H economies have a notably higher proportion of public current expenditure on tertiary education (average 26.6 percent), whereas the other two groups (L and M) have similar rates of about 11-14 percent. Correlating the tertiary GERs with the proportion of public current expenditure shows the extent of unequal access to education, if compared with the GER in tertiary education. For example, in the L countries the tertiary sector, which accounts for only 3.1 percent of the average GER, consumes 11.2 percent of the average public current expenditure. Looking at individual countries, in Indonesia, the tertiary GER is only 11.3 percent but accounts for 25.1 percent of public current expenditure on education. The contrast in Nepal is even greater: 4.7 percent of tertiary GER accounts for 17.9 percent of public current expenditure (see Appendix 1, Table A1.9). This suggests that in countries with low and medium HDI and GNP per capita, access to tertiary education remains a privilege for a small proportion of people, and they consume a disproportionately high amount of education expenditure. This means that only the richest can afford tertiary education in most DMCs. It may also mean that public resources are inequitably given to a small group of people, further hindering the universalization of education at the secondary level (Table 41).

Table 40: Average Gross Enrollment Rate by Level of Education and Grouping, 1996
(percent)

Grouping	Primary education	Secondary education	Tertiary education
L	87.8	26.9	3.1
M	102.9	55.2	13.2
H	95.1	83.1	42.3

Note: L, M, and H refer to country groupings with low, middle, and high HDI and GNP per capita respectively.

Source: Appendix 1, Table A1.9.

Access and Equity in Education and Earned Income Share by Gender

Table 42 shows that the GDI ranking is positively correlated with the HDI ranking, i.e., the lower the HDI, the lower the GDI. However, their relationship with GEM is less clear. For example, Bangladesh (83) and the Republic of Korea (78) have similar GEM ranks, but Bangladesh has extremely low HDI (150) and GDI (123) ranks, whereas the Republic of Korea has very high HDI (30) and GDI (30) ranks. This means that despite economic development, there has not been much improvement in female empowerment in the Republic of Korea. However, this does not mean that the situation of female empowerment is very good either, as the lowest rank in the *Human Development Report 1999* is 102, implying that Bangladesh's GEM is close to the bottom of all those countries being ranked. Considering DMCs as a whole, except for a few countries with relatively high ranks (such as Singapore 32, PRC 40, Philippines 45, and Malaysia 52), the GEM ranks of DMCs are within the range of 70-100 which is quite near the bottom of the GEM ranking (see Appendix 1, Table A1.5). This suggests that the general sociocultural context in DMCs is not favorable for female empowerment.

Looking at the combined average GER, in which primary, secondary, and tertiary levels of education are included, within country groupings, it is found that there is in general parity in enrollments between males and females in the M and H economies. A clearer disparity is found among the L countries, with a male/female rate of 1.4. Signified with a very low GEM rank (101), females'

Table 41: Average Proportion of Public Current Expenditure on Higher Education by Grouping
(percent)

Grouping	Average GER in higher education	Average proportion of public current expenditure on higher education (% of all levels)
L	3.1	11.2
M	13.2	13.5
H	42.3	26.6

Note: L, M, and H refer to country groupings with low, middle, and high HDI and GNP per capita respectively.

Source: Appendix 1, Table A1.9.

Table 42: Average Male/Female Rate of Combined GER and Earned Income Share by Grouping, 1997

Grouping	Range of HDI Rank 1997	Range of GDI Rank 1997	Range of GEM Rank 1997	Average combined GER, M/F 1997[a]	Average earned income share, M/F 1995
L	140-150	115-123	around 83	1.4	2.2
M	56-138	52-116	45-101	1.1	1.9
H	22-30	22-30	32-78	1.0	2.5

Note: L, M, and H refer to country groupings with low, middle, and high HDI and GNP per capita respectively.
[a] Including primary, secondary, and tertiary levels of education.

Source: Appendix 1, Table A1.5.

Table 43: Average Male/Female Rate of GER by Level of Education and Grouping, 1996

Grouping	Primary	Secondary	Tertiary
L	1.4	2.0	3.2
M	1.1	1.1	1.5
H	1.0	1.0	1.3

Note: L, M, and H refer to country groupings with low, middle, and high HDI and GNP per capita respectively.

Source: Appendix 1, Table A1.10.

enrollment chance in Pakistan is only half that of the males.

The average earned income share between males and females is not much different between the L and H economies, where males' income share percentage ratio is 2.2 and 2.5 times, respectively, that of females. The largest gap found in the L countries is in Bangladesh (3.3 times), while that in the H economies is in Hong Kong, China (2.9 times) (see Appendix 1, Table A1.5). Despite economic development, data suggest that empowerment of women in some respects in some H economies is lower than that in some M countries (Table 42).

Table 43 shows that the gender gap in GER in the L countries is wider than in the M and H economies at all levels of education. The disparity in enrollments is especially large at the tertiary level in the L countries, with an average male/female rate of 3.2. Such an obvious average gender gap in enrollments in the L countries is attributable to a wide gap in Bangladesh, where the male/female enrollment rate is 5.4. Moreover, while approaching parity at primary and secondary schooling in the M and H economies, gender disparity remains at the tertiary level (see Appendix 1, Table A1.10).

Labor Force, Urban/Rural Population Distribution, and Education

Labor Force and Rural Population

Table 44 shows a great contrast in the proportion of the rural population in different country groupings: as high as 83.2 percent in the L countries but as low as 7.3 percent in the H economies. This coincides with the average proportion of GDP share of agriculture in the respective country groupings: 38.8 percent in the L countries and 2 percent in the H economies. What this means is that if the urban-rural disparity is a significant problem today, this is a widespread problem in DMCs, as the H economies account for an extremely small proportion of DMCs.

Illiteracy, Rural Population, and Labor Force in Agriculture

The adult illiteracy rate varies significantly between country groups. More than half of the adult population is illiterate in the L countries. However, average adult illiteracy is only 15.2 percent in the M countries and 6.2 percent in the H economies. Combining the adult illiterate rates with the proportion of rural population, it is easy to see that illiteracy is pervasive in countries that have large proportions of a rural population and agricultural labor force (Table 44).

Illiteracy rates are high among both males and females in the L countries. This indicates that the gender gap in illiteracy is the most modest among DMCs. In contrast, despite extremely low adult illiteracy rates in the H economies, the gender gap is the widest among DMCs. Comparing the different country groupings, the L countries have the widest gender gap in GERs but the narrowest in illiteracy. The H economies, on the other hand, have the narrowest gender gap in GERs but the widest in adult illiteracy. This means that in the low-HDI-low-GDI countries, both males and females, share similar rates of illiteracy; but once there is an opportunity for education, boys have much more opportunities than girls. In the H economies, although there are more or less equal education opportunities at the school level, females still account for a large proportion of illiterate people (see Appendix 1, Table A1.11).

Female Political and Economic Participation

Despite generally low GEM ranks in DMCs, there are differences in females' life chances beyond education between country groupings. However, like GEM ranking, women's empowerment in a society may not have a direct linkage to the country's economic or human development. Table 45 shows that women occupy less than 10 percent of parliamentary seats in DMCs. The proportion of women in parliament is more or less the same in the L, M, and H economies. However, women's representation in parliament is notably low in the H economies, comprising only 4.3 percent of the seats. Looking at the male/ female rate in parliament, while males exceed females by 9-12 times in the other two country groupings, it is 22.5 times in the H economies. However, the picture of female participation in administrative and managerial occupations is totally reversed. While females account for only 5 percent in administrative and managerial occupations in the L countries, the rate is 13 percent in the

Table 44: Average Rural Population, Illiteracy Rate, and Labor Force in Agriculture by Grouping
(percent)

Grouping	Average rural population 1997	Average GDI share of agriculture 1997	Average labor force in agriculture		Average labor force in industry		Average adult illiteracy rate estimate 1995[a]			
			1970	1990	1970	1990	Total	M	F	F/M
L	83.2	38.8	88.5	82.8	3.8	5.8	60.8	47.4	74.5	1.6
M	66.4	26.7	62.6	52.2	14.2	18.0	15.2	10.0	19.3	1.9
H	7.3	2.0	18.7	6.3	35.0	36.0	6.2	2.9	9.6	3.7

Note: L, M, and H refer to country groupings with low, middle, and high HDI and GNP per capita respectively.
[a] Data refer to population 15 years old and above.

Source: Appendix 1, Table A1.11.

Table 45: Political and Economic Participation of Women by Grouping

Grouping	Range of GDI Rank 1997	Seats held in parliament 1999		Administrative & manager 1992-1996		Professional & technical workers 1992-1996		Sales & service workers 1992-1996		Clerical workers 1992-1996	
		F%	M/F	F%	M/F	F%	M/F	F%	M/F	F%	M/F
L	115-123	9.2	9.9	5.0	19.0	23.0	3.3	4.0	24.0	46.0	1.2
M	52-116	7.5	12.3	12.8	6.8	37.5	1.7	41.1	1.4	40.2	1.5
H	22-30	4.3	22.5	13.0	6.7	35.7	1.8	47.3	1.1	66.7	0.5

Note: L, M, and H refer to country groupings with low, middle, and high HDI and GNP per capita respectively.

Source: Appendix 1, Table A1.2.

Table 46: Participation of Women in Teaching Profession by Grouping, 1996

Grouping	Primary Education			Secondary education			Tertiary education		
	M%	F%	M/F	M%	F%	M/F	M%	F%	M/F
L	80.0	20.0	4.0	62.0	38.0	1.6	71.0	29.0	2.4
M	43.9	56.1	0.8	46.5	53.5	0.9	70.8	29.3	2.4
H	36.7	63.3	0.6	55.5	44.5	1.2	73.3	26.7	2.8

Note: L, M, and H refer to country groupings with low, middle, and high HDI and GNP per capita respectively.

Source: Appendix 1, Table A1.12.

other two groups. This may mean that while women are politically active in the low HDI and GDI countries, they are economically and administratively passive; this pattern is reversed in the H economies. However, this does not necessarily mean high gender empowerment in the L countries. The literature on gender studies points out that women who climb to power do not necessarily devote their efforts to raising the sociopolitical status of females, but are usually more interested in securing their own power in their political system.

Referring to other occupational categories, there seems to be parity in gender distribution. However, teaching is regarded as a professional job that comprises mainly women. If teachers are excluded from the professional category, women may be much less represented in professional occupations. However, as revealed in Table 46, such representation is concentrated in primary and secondary levels of education only. In both M and H country groupings, females' participation rates in teaching at the tertiary level drops conspicuously. Moreover, for all occupational categories except political participation, gender disparity is more notable in the L countries than the other country groupings. This may be due to a general low level of education attainments in South Asia.

High HDI and Low HDI Economies Compared: Hong Kong, China and the Lao PDR

After looking at country groupings in general, it may be useful to compare two individual economies. Hong Kong, China and the Lao PDR are chosen for this purpose, as the former is an economy in Group H with high HDI and GDI, and is mainly urban and industrial. In contrast, the Lao PDR is an L country, with low HDI and GDI. It is mainly an agrarian economy, with a large rural population.

Table 47 shows that males exceed females in nearly all types of occupations except clerks in Hong Kong, China and elementary occupations in the Lao PDR. The two occupations in which females occupy higher proportions are actually humble jobs in both societies. Clerical jobs are generally regarded as the new working class job in an industrial society, and elementary occupations are obviously those of low social status. Males exceed females to the greatest extent in administrative and managerial positions, by four times in Hong Kong, China and nine times in the Lao PDR. For other occupations, the male/female ratio is mostly about 2:1. This further illustrates the fact that, despite the state of economic development, females are still far from having equal life chances to males.

Table 48 compares the proportion of females in various tertiary level fields of study in Hong Kong, China and the Lao PDR. Males exceed females in nearly all fields of study in the Lao PDR, whereas the pattern is reversed in Hong Kong, China. In Hong Kong, China, females are the majority particularly in the fields of education, humanities, and social sciences, whereas there is more or less parity in trade and natural sciences. However, males far exceed females in engineering and architecture. This is a clear demonstration of gender stereotyping in the fields of study. As the outlets of humanities and social sciences are usually teachers and social workers, females are mainly clustered in the "female subjects." In subjects that can lead to better professional or high-income jobs, the proportion of male enrollments is increased.

In contrast, the Lao PDR figures show an overall domination of males in tertiary enrollments. Apart from education, social sciences, and natural science, males exceed females in most fields of study from two to seven times. It is another demonstration of male dominance in tertiary enrollments in a low HDI and GDI economy.

Table 47: Employment by Occupation and Male/Female Rate in Hong Kong, China and the Lao PDR, 1992

	Employment, Male/Female Rate	
Occupation	*Hong Kong, China*	*Lao PDR*
Mangers and administrators	4.0	9.1
Professionals	2.2	2.1
Service workers and shop sales workers	1.8	—
Plant and machine operators and assemblers	1.8	2.7
Elementary occupation	1.3	0.6
Clerks	0.5	1.0
Farm workers	—	1.1

— Data not available.

Sources: Netherlands Economic Institute 1995, 17, 48; Westwood, Mehrain, and Cheung 1995, 74.

Table 48: Proportions of Females in Tertiary Level Fields of Study in Hong Kong, China and the Lao PDR, 1994

Field of study	Hong Kong, China		Lao PDR	
	Female (%)	Male/ Female	Female (%)	Male/ Female
Education	62.8	0.59	40.1	1.49
Humanities	75.5	0.32	32.8	2.05
Social sciences	66.5	0.51	45.1	1.21
Business administration	54.3	0.84	—	—
Trade	51.3	0.95	—	—
Natural science	—	—	49.3	1.03
Engineering	6.0	15.70	18.0	4.56
Architecture	21.0	3.76	12.7	6.88

— Data not available.

Source: UNESCO, Division of Statistics 1999.

Policy Implications

The pattern presented above highlights the following three aspects that need attention from policymakers:

(i) *Efforts to expand secondary schooling and consolidate primary schooling.* Universal primary education has generally been achieved in DMCs, but about half of the children in the population have no access to secondary education in the countries with medium-low income and HDI. DMCs should aim to expand access to secondary schooling for all. At the primary level, the major task is to reduce dropouts and increase retention. Investment in basic education is still a priority for the medium-low income DMCs, not only to consolidate access but also as a means to consolidate equity in terms of resource distribution. The NIEs and ASEAN countries spend most on primary education, then on the secondary schools, and the least on higher education (Bautista 1990, 49). As argued above, the largest group of income poor is likely to benefit in basic education rather than higher education.

(ii) *The gender gap at higher levels of education.* The obvious gender gap from secondary education onward needs attention. Associated with this, there appears a need to attend to the sociocultural biases against females in attending schools, in getting equal pay, and in participating in government administration. In sum, there appears to be a need for empowerment of females in DMCs.

(iii) *The problem of rural education.* The L and M countries have much higher average rural populations than the three H economies. These rural populations still suffer from insufficient access to schooling, and addressing the issue of rural education is much needed in most DMCs.

Conclusion

The above review suggests that access and equity in education continue to be a significant problem in DMCs, despite general economic and human development. The major facets of inequity, in terms of gender, income, region, and ethnicity, are pervasive. This is especially the case in South Asia, where most countries have low HDI, GDI, and GNP per capita. This underlines the point made at the beginning of the booklet that inequity has a strong association with human poverty, and is not necessarily associated with high economic growth.

Below is a summary of the observations drawn from the analysis. The issues identified represent problems faced by DMCs, and additional resources and extra efforts are required to enhance access and equity in education in these countries.

Gender-Related Equity

In respect to gender perspectives, the major observations are:

(I)   In most DMCs, the proportion of female illiterates is larger than that of male illiterates. In many countries, the proportion of female illiterates has grown.

(ii)   Primary gross enrollments in general approached gender parity by the 1980s.

(iii) About half the DMCs approached gender parity in secondary enrollments in the 1990s. Among DMCs with higher male enrollments, the male/female ratios are mostly below 2:1, with the exception of a few South Asian countries.

(iv)   Gender disparity is more obvious in tertiary enrollments and favorable on the male side, with the exception of a few East and Southeast Asian countries. The largest gap between male and female was 5:4 in Bangladesh.

(v)   There is also gender stereotyping in tertiary education, with females focusing on humanities and social sciences while males focus on mathematics, science, engineering, and architecture. Subjects that lead to a better prospect of professional and economic status are still dominated by men.

(vi)   In terms of economic and political participation in society, females are severely underrepresented in parliamentary seats or ministerial positions, as well as managerial positions. They are quite well represented in

74

professional occupations, but may be concentrated in the field of education.

(vii) There is a clear gender gap in wages, with females sharing only 35 to 40 percent of the earned income. But despite this disparity, the impact of additional schooling on earnings is higher for females than males.

(viii) All DMCs have GEM values lower than their HDI and GDI values.

(ix) While there is a relationship between HDI and GDI, there is no relationship between HDI, GDI, and GEM. This implies that economic and human development does not necessarily link to female empowerment. This fact further suggests that economic development is not a sufficient boost for female empowerment, and attention should be given to the sociocultural dimension of female empowerment.

Income-Related Equity

In respect to income-related equity, the major observations are:

(i) South Asia has the highest incidence of income poverty, and is home to one third of the income poor in the developing countries. However, the NIEs have achieved a large reduction of income poverty.

(ii) The proportion of the income poor has declined in the last two decades, but the number of income poor has increased.

(iii) The Gini index in many DMCs falls within the range of 30 and 40. Income inequality has declined, but some societies have experienced widened income inequality. Indonesia and Hong Kong, China are in the latter category.

(iv) Enrollment rates of the income poor are notably lower than those of the nonpoor; and the higher the level of education, the wider the gap between the poor and the nonpoor.

(v) Poor females are the most vulnerable in school nonattendance and noncompletion.

(vi) Additional household financial contributions to education are becoming a more notable phenomenon. This creates an additional barrier for the income poor to attend schools.

(vii) The concept of "low payoff, high opportunity costs" constitutes a significant barrier to education not only among the income poor in rural areas, but also in fast-growing areas such as parts of the PRC.

Region-Related Equity

In respect to region-related equity, the major observations are:

(i) Region-related equity is inseparable from gender and income equity. In this sense, the most disadvantaged group in terms of access to education is poor rural girls.

(ii)   Notable gaps persist in literacy, enrollment, and school completion rates between urban and rural areas.

(iii)   The gap is even more conspicuous among females. For example, in Afghanistan the urban female literacy rate is 9.5 times higher than the rural female rate.

(iv)   The urban-rural gap is also wide in school completion rates. It has been as great as 45.9 times in Pakistan and 15.6 times in Nepal.

(v)   A few countries have achieved close to equal enrollment rates between urban and rural areas. However, even in these countries the gap becomes evident at the tertiary level, especially among females.

(vi)   Other types of disparities can be related to regional differences based on economic growth, proximity to the political center, and historical significance of the regions.

(vii)   Decentralization and liberalization of economy can aggravate regional disparities in economic development and in education enrollments.

(viii) Migration of the labor force to more prosperous urban regions has created pressures on education. The migration of males to urban regions leaves females behind, putting pressure on rural enrollments for females, while large floating populations create pressure on education provisions for the children of such populations in major cities. This has been evident, for example, in Guangzhou and Shanghai in the PRC.

(ix)   Different regional economic conditions have led to different education expenditures between regions, therefore creating disparities in education resources and facilities between regions.

(x)   Conditions of schools in rural regions are generally poor, and they may not offer complete years of schooling, even at the primary level.

(xi)   The issue of urban poverty is increasingly felt in Asia, and there is evidence that the demand for household financial contributions to education is higher in urban areas than rural areas.

Sociocultural-Related Equity

In respect to sociocultural-related equity, the major observations are:

(i)   Inequity is by and large influenced by sociocultural perceptions and traditions, particularly in relation to gender.

(ii)   While some minorities are quite successful, for example, the Chinese outside the PRC and the Koreans in the PRC, in most cases ethnic minorities are disadvantaged in terms both of enrollments and of school completion. Moreover, the higher the level of education, the smaller the proportion of the minorities in school. Subtle tensions between ethnic groups may pose a problem for further advancement of the minorities in society.

(iii)   In most cases, minorities reside in remote areas and in rural areas, and are among the income poor. As the areas in which they reside are unfavorable for economic development, they tend to suffer long-term poverty.

(iv) In addition to language, the low self-esteem of the minorities may affect their education achievements.

(v) Gender disparities are largely a sociocultural issue: where they have to choose, families will give priority to boys for education.

(vi) The dominance of the patriarchal society continues to pose difficulties for females to change their life chances, despite the state of the economy, and despite the levels of education attainment.

(vii) Gender stereotyping in the curriculum and in the choice of fields of study continues to sustain difficulties for females to enhance their life chances.

Patterns of Access and Equity by Country Groupings

Grouping of DMCs by high-HDI-high-GDI, medium-HDI-medium-GDI and low-HDI-low-GDI reveals some patterns in access and equity:

(i) Universal primary education has generally been achieved in DMCs, but about half of the children have no access to secondary education in the medium-low HDI and GNP per capita countries, and tertiary education is a privilege for a very small proportion of people in these countries.

(ii) In terms of literacy and education enrollments, the high-HDI-high-GDI economies have distinctly higher rates than other DMCs.

(iii) In relation to public current expenditure, the lower the ranking in the HDI and GDI, the higher the proportion of public current expenditure on tertiary education, further illustrating that a small group of privileged students are consuming a relatively large proportion of education spending in low-performing economies. On the one hand this pattern demonstrates a large extent of inequity in low-performing economies; on the other it implies that only the rich can afford higher levels of education.

(iv) In terms of gender-related equity, despite DMCs all having low GEM ranks compared with other parts of the world, the NIEs in general have higher GEM ranks than the low-performing economies. However, individual DMCs may have significant deviations. For example, the Republic of Korea has very high HDI and GDI ranks but a very low GEM rank. In contrast, the PRC and Philippines have relatively low HDI and GDI ranks but relatively high GEM ranks. This also implies that gender empowerment relies not only on the economy, but also on the willpower of the government and the capacity of society to change sociocultural perceptions.

(v) The gender gap in income share may not be correlated with a country's HDI, GDI, or GNP per capita ranks. The Group L and H economies have a larger gender gap in income share than the Group M economies.

(vi)   In low-performing economies, the gender gap is low in illiteracy but wide in enrollments; the pattern is reversed in NIEs. This implies that in poor countries, both genders may suffer similarly when there is no chance for education. However, when there is a chance for education, the chance goes to the boys.

(vii) The Group L and M countries have average proportions of rural population much higher than the three Group H economies, implying that if rural education is a problem at all, it is a pervasive problem in DMCs.

(viii) In terms of political and economic participation, while females in the medium- and low-performing economies can be active politically, they are passive economically and administratively. However, in the NIEs, females' empowerment capability is not enhanced as their proportion in parliamentary seats is the lowest among the three country groupings.

The above observations suggest that "education for all" will continue to be an agenda item in Asia, and that projects to improve education in disadvantaged contexts should be extended to cover more areas in the medium- and low-performing economies that constitute the majority of DMCs. Countries in South Asia should receive greater attention and external help for improvement in their education provision. In addition to economic strengthening, efforts have to be made to change the sociocultural context into one favorable to the disadvantaged.

The improvement of access and equity in education requires political will and commitment. No doubt, a country's general improvement in economic conditions can be helpful for reducing poverty and improving the general living conditions and life chances of the disadvantaged. However, this does not necessarily lead to such an outcome. *Emerging Asia* (ADB 1997, 268) points out that economic growth does not explain all of Asia's diversity. Some countries and regions with relatively low incomes per person have disproportionately high standards of health, education, and nutrition.

Note on the Author

W.O. Lee is Professor and Dean of the School of Foundations in Education, and Head of the Centre for Citizenship Education, at the Hong Kong Institute of Education. He has previously served in the Faculty of Education at the University of Hong Kong, as Associate Dean of Education and Director of the Comparative Education Research Centre. He is also a past president of the Comparative Education Society of Hong Kong. He has published widely in the areas of comparative education, with foci on values education and socio-cultural perspectives. His books include *Social Change and Educational Problems in Japan, Singapore and Hong Kong* (1991), *Social Change and Educational Development: Mainland China, Taiwan and Hong Kong* (co-edited 1995), and *Education and Political Transition: Perspectives and Dimensions in East Asia* (co-edited 1997). Address: School of Foundations in Education, Hong Kong Institute of Education, 10 Lo Ping Road, Taipo, Hong Kong, China. E-mail: wolee@ied.edu.hk.

The author expresses gratitude to Sara Wong for her valuable help in the preparation of this booklet.

References

Asian Development Bank (ADB). 1993. *Gender Indicators of Developing Asian and Pacific Countries*. Manila: ADB.

―――. 1994a. *Framework and Criteria for the Appraisal and Socioeconomic Justification of Education Projects*. Manila: ADB.

―――. 1994b. *Women in Development: Issues, Challenges and Strategies in Asia and the Pacific*. Manila: ADB.

―――. 1995. *Financing Human Development: Lessons from Advanced Asian Economies*. Manila: ADB.

―――. 1996a. *Human Development: Cross-cutting Concerns*. Cambodia Studies Series. Manila: ADB.

―――. 1996b. *Lao PDR Human Development: Future Strategic Directions*. Manila: ADB.

―――. 1996c. *The National Policy for Women: Cambodia*. Manila: ADB.

―――. 1996d. *Sociocultural Issues and Economic Development in the Pacific Islands*. Manila: ADB.

―――. 1996e. *Viet Nam: Human Development Perspectives*. Manila: ADB.

―――. 1997. *Emerging Asia: Changes and Challenges*. Manila: ADB

―――. 1999. *Annual Report 1998*. Manila. ADB.

Dajracharya, H.R., Thapa, B.K., and Chitrakar, R. 1997. *Trends, Issues and Policies in Education of Nepal: A Country Case Study*. Manila: ADB.

Balisacan, A. 1996. Philippines. In *Rural Poverty in Developing Asia*. Vol.2, edited by M.G. Quibria. Manila: ADB.

Bauer, A., Green, D., and Kuehnast, K. 1997. *Women and Gender Relations: The Kyrgyz Republic in Transition*. Manila: ADB.

Bautista, R.M. 1990. *Poverty reduction, Economic Growth and Development Policy in East Asia*. Canberra: National Centre for Development Studies, Australian National University.

Bray, M. 1996. *Counting the Full Cost: Parental and Community Financing of Education in East Asia*. Washington, DC: The World Bank in collaboration with UNICEF.

―――. 2002. *The Costs and Financing of Education: Trends and Policy Implications*. Series "Education in Developing Asia." Manila: Asian Development Bank, and Hong Kong: Comparative Education Research Centre, University of Hong Kong.

Chagnon, J. 1996. *Women in Development: Lao PDR*. Manila: ADB.

Chang, S.M. 1991. Korea. Paper presented at the Regional Seminar on the Urban Poor and Basic Infrastructure held by ADB and the World Bank's Economic Development Institute, 22-28 January, Manila.

Cheng, K.M. 1995. Education, Decentralisation and Regional Disparity in China. In *Social Change and Educational Development: Mainland China, Taiwan and Hong Kong*, edited by G.A. Postiglione and W.O. Lee. Hong Kong: Centre of Asian Studies, University of Hong Kong.

China Education Statistical Yearbook. 1994. Beijing: People's Education Press.

Chou, B.E. 1994. Changing Patterns of Women's Employment in Taiwan, 1966-1988. In *The Other Taiwan: 1945 to the Present*, edited by M.A. Rubinstein. New York: M.E. Sharpe.

Chowdhury, K.P. 1997. Bangladesh. In *Asian Higher Education: An International Handbook and Reference Guide,* edited by G.A. Postiglione and G.C.L. Mak. Westport: Greenwood Press.

Chuard, D., and Mingat, A. 1996a. *Analysis of Dropout and Student Learning in Primary Education in Bhutan.* Manila: ADB.

————. 1996b. *Analysis of Dropout and Student Learning in Primary Education in South Asia: Bangladesh, Bhutan, Nepal and Pakistan.* Manila: ADB.

Chung, K.W., and Oh, N.W. 1996. Republic of Korea. In *Rural Poverty in Developing Asia.* Vol. 2, edited by M.G. Quibria. Manila: ADB.

Council on Educational Reform. 1995. *Council Report No. 1.* Taipei: Council on Educational Reform, Executive Yuan. (In Chinese)

Cui, G.H. 1995. Development of Shanghai and the Yangtze Delta. In *Chinese Cities and China's Development: A Preview of the Future Role of Hong Kong,* edited by A.G.O. Yeh and C.K. Mak. Hong Kong: Centre of Urban Planning and Environmental Management, University of Hong Kong.

Daroesman, R. 1985. Indonesia. In *Unemployment, Schooling and Training in Developing Countries: Tanzania, Egypt, the Philippines and Indonesia,* edited by M. Leonor. London: Croom Helm.

Emberson-Bain, A. 1995. *Women in Development: Kiribati.* Manila: ADB.

Gertler, P.J., and Rahman, O. 1994. Social Infrastructure and Urban Poverty. In *Urban Poverty in Asia: A Survey of Critical Issues,* edited by E.N. Pernia. Hong Kong: Oxford University Press.

Hayhoe, R. 1995. Student Enrolment and Job Assignment Issues in China. In *Social Change and Educational Development: Mainland China, Taiwan and Hong Kong,* edited by G.A. Postiglione and W.O. Lee. Hong Kong: Centre of Asian Studies, University of Hong Kong.

Hook, B., and Lee, W.O. 1998. Human Resources. In *Beijing and Tianjin.* Series "Regional Development in China." Vol.4, edited by B. Hook. Hong Kong: Oxford University Press.

Hossain, M., Mannab, R., Rahman, H.Z., and Sen, B. 1994. Bangladesh. In *Rural Poverty in Developing Asia.* Vol. 1, edited by M.G. Quibria. Manila: ADB.

Hu, A., Wang, S.G., and Kang, X.G. 1995. *Regional Disparities in China.* Shenyang: Liaoning People's Press. (In Chinese)

Indonesia, Ministry of Education and Culture. 1997. *Education Development in Indonesia.* Jakarta: Ministry of Education and Culture.

Jayaweera, S. 1991. *Women in Development: Sri Lanka.* Manila: ADB.

Kajima, Y. 1995. *Women in Development: Mongolia.* Manila: ADB.

Krongkaew, M., Tinakorn, P., and Suphachalasai, S. 1996. Thailand. In *Rural Poverty in Developing Asia.* Vol. 2, edited by M.G. Quibria. Manila: ADB.

Lee, M.N.N. 1997. Malaysia. In *Asian Higher Education: An International Handbook and Reference Guide,* edited by G.A. Postiglione and G.C.L. Mak. Westport: Greenwood Press.

Lee, W.O. 1991. *Social Change and Educational Problems in Japan, Singapore and Hong Kong.* London: Macmillan.

Lee, W.O., and Li, Z. 1995. Education, Development and Regional Disparity in Guangzhou. In *Social Change and Educational Development: Mainland China, Taiwan and Hong Kong,* edited by G.A. Postiglione and W.O. Lee. Hong Kong: Centre of Asian Studies, University of Hong Kong.

Lewin, K.M. 1996. *Access to Education in Emerging Asia: Trends, Challenges and Policy Options.* Manila: ADB.

Liu, P.W., Wong, R.Y.C., Sung, Y.W., and Lau, P.K. 1992. *China's Economic Reform and Development Strategy of Pearl River Delta.* Hong Kong: Nanyang Commercial Bank Ltd.

Lucas, R.E.B., and Verry, D.W. 1996. Growth and Income Distribution. *International Labour Review* 35(5):553-75.

Lui, H.K. 1997. *Income Inequality and Economic Development.* Series "The Hong Kong Economic Policy Studies." Hong Kong: City University of Hong Kong Press.

Ma, C.F. 1991. *A Research on the Image of Father in Primary School and Kindergarten in Hong Kong.* Hong Kong: Hong Kong Christian Service. (In Chinese)

Mackerras, C. 1995. *China's Minority Cultures.* New York: St. Martin's Press.

Maitra, T. 1985. *Public Services in India.* Delhi: Mittal.

McDonald, M. 1995. *Women in Development: Viet Nam.* Manila: ADB.

Mendez, P.P. 1990. Participation of Women in Higher Education in the Philippines. In *Women's Participation in Higher Education: China, Nepal and the Philippines.* Bangkok: UNESCO Principal Regional Office for Asia and the Pacific.

Mingat, A., and Chuard, D. 1996. *Analysis of Drop-out and Student Learning in Primary Education in Pakistan.* Manila: ADB.

Netherlands Economic Institute. 1995. *Strengthening Labour Market Monitoring and Analysis in Lao PDR (Final Report).* Rotterdam, The Netherlands: Netherlands Economic Institute.

Niu, X.D. 1993. Gender Inequality in Chinese Education. *Education and Society* 11(2):19-27.

Philippines, Government of the. 1997. *Making Education Work. Book One: Areas of Concern in Philippine Education.* Vol. 3: Sectoral Targets and Functional Linkages. Manila.

Postiglione, G.A. 1992. The Implications of Modernization for the Education of China's National Minorities. In *Education and Modernization: The Chinese Experience,* edited by R. Hayhoe. Oxford: Pergamon Press.

Postiglione, G.A., Teng, X., and Ai, Y.P. 1995. Basic Education and School Discontinuation in National Minority Border Regions of China. In *Social Change and Educational Development: Mainland China, Taiwan and Hong*

Kong, edited by G.A. Postiglione and W.O. Lee. Hong Kong: Centre of Asian Studies, University of Hong Kong.

Quibria, M.G. 1994. *Rural Poverty in Developing Asia*. Vol.1. Manila: ADB.

———. 1996. *Rural Poverty in Developing Asia*. Vol.2. Manila: ADB.

Rohlen, T. 1981. Education: Policies and Prospects. In *Koreans in Japan: Ethnic Conflict and Accommodation*, edited by C. Lee and G. Devos. Los Angeles: University of California Press.

Selvaratnam, V. 1987. *Ethnicity, Inequality and Higher Education in Peninsular Malaysia: The Sociological Implication*. Singapore: Department of Sociology, National University of Singapore.

Shi, Jinghuan. 1995. China's Cultural Tradition and Women's Participation in Education. In *Social Change and Educational Development: Mainland China, Taiwan and Hong Kong*, edited by G.A. Postiglione and W.O. Lee. Hong Kong: Centre of Asian Studies, University of Hong Kong.

Shrestha, P., Pradhan, K.M., Ghimier, S., and Singh, S. 1990. Participation of Women in Higher Education in Nepal. In *Women's Participation in Higher Education: China, Nepal and the Philippines*. Bangkok: UNESCO Principal Regional Office for Asia and the Pacific.

Sun, T., and Liang, S. 1997. Study on the Transfer of Agricultural Surplus Labour Forces in Central China. In *Regional Economic Development Policy in China*, edited by T. Maruya. Tokyo: Institute of Developing Economies.

Tan, S.V. 1993. *The Education of Chinese in the Philippines and Koreans in Japan*. M.A. Dissertation, Hong Kong: University of Hong Kong.

Thapa, B. K. 1996. *Drop-out of Primary Students in Nepal*. Manila: ADB.

Tjondronegoro, S.M.P., Soejono, R., and Hardjono, J. 1996. Indonesia. In *Rural Poverty in Developing Asia*. Vol.2, edited by M.G. Quibria. Manila: ADB.

Tilak, J.B.G. 1994. *Education for Development in Asia*. New Delhi: Sage Publications.

———. 1995. *How Free is "Free" Primary Education in India?* Occasional Paper 21. New Delhi: National Institute of Educational Planning and Administration.

Todaro, M.P. 1997. *Economic Development*. London: Longman.

United Nations. 1995. *Trends, Patterns and Implications of Rural-Urban Migration in India, Nepal and Thailand*. New York: United Nations.

United Nations Development Programme (UNDP). 1996. *Human Development Report 1996*. New York: Oxford University Press for the United Nations Development Programme.

———. 1997. *Human Development Report 1997*. New York: Oxford University Press for the United Nations Development Programme.

———. 1998. *Human Development Report 1998*. New York: Oxford University Press for the United Nations Development Programme.

———. 1999. *Human Development Report 1999*. New York: Oxford University Press for the United Nations Development Programme.

United Nations Educational, Scientific and Cultural Organization (UNESCO), Division of Statistics. 1993. Development of Education in Asia and the

Pacific: A Statistical Review. Document presented at the Sixth Regional Conference of Ministers of Education and those Responsible for Economic Planning in Asia and the Pacific, Kuala Lumpur, 21-24 June.

————. 1999. *World Education Indicators.* http://www.unescostat.unesco.org/indicator.

United Nations Educational, Scientific and Cultural Organization, Principal Regional Office for Asia and the Pacific (UNESCO-PROAP). 1996. *Mid-decade Review of Education for All in South Asia.* Bangkok: UNESCO Principal Regional Office for Asia and the Pacific.

Walton, M. 1990. Combating Poverty: Experience and Prospects. *Finance and Development* (September):2-5.

Westwood, R., Mehrain, T., and Cheung, F. 1995. *Gender and Society in Hong Kong: A Statistical Profile.* Hong Kong: The Chinese University Press.

World Bank. 1993. *The East Asian Miracle: Economic Growth and Public Policy.* New York: Oxford University Press.

————. 1996a. *China. Third Basic Education Project.* Report No. 15099-CHA. East Asia and Pacific Regional Office, China and Mongolia Department, Washington, DC.

————. 1996b. *Indonesia: Dimensions of Growth.* Report No. 15383-IND. East Asia and Pacific Regional Office, Country Department III, Washington, DC.

————. 1999. *World Development Indicators 1999.* Washington, DC: World Bank.

World Conference on Education for All (WCEFA). 1990. *World Declaration on Education for All.* New York; WCFFA Inter-Agency Commission.

Wu, D.G. 1995. *A Study of Tibet's Educational Reform and Development.* Kunming: Yunnan Education. (In Chinese)

Yang, H.H. 1992. *Rural Development and its Impact on Rural Education in China.* M.Ed. Dissertation, Edmonton: University of Alberta.

Yau, B.L.L., and Luk, H.K. 1990. Gender Roles as Defined in Current Social Studies Textbooks at the Junior Secondary Level in Hong Kong. In *Women and Education in China, Hong Kong and Taiwan.* New York: Comparative Education Center, State University of New York at Buffalo.

Yeh, A.G.O. 1995. Urbanization Trend in China - Coastal, River and Interior Cities in China's Development. In *Chinese Cities and China's Development: A Preview of the Future Role of Hong Kong,* edited by A.G.O. Yeh and C.K. Mak. Hong Kong: Centre of Urban Planning and Environmental Management, University of Hong Kong.

Zhao Z.Y., Chen, S.Q., and Liu, H.Y. 1993. Report on the Survey of the Value Orientations of the Adolescent Students of Three Ethnic Groups in China. *Studies in Ethnic Education* 1:34-44. (In Chinese)

Appendix 1: Tables

Table A1.1: Population that Have Completed Secondary School by Gender in DMCs

Economy	Circa 1970			Circa 1980			Latest		
	F%	M%	M/F	F%	M%	M/F	F%	M%	M/F
Afghanistan	0.4	2.3	5.8	0.7	6.9	9.9	—	—	—
Bangladesh	—	—	—	1.3	8.0	6.1	—	—	—
Nepal	—	—	—	1.3	7.3	5.6	—	—	—
Pakistan	—	—	—	3.1	10.6	3.4	—	—	—
India	2.0	8.2	4.1	4.2	13.2	3.1	—	—	—
Maldives	—	—	—	0.8	2.4	3.0	1.7	1.8	1.1
Fiji Islands	—	—	—	1.1	2.7	2.5	4.5	6.3	1.4
Indonesia	1.5	3.9	2.6	4.0	8.2	2.1	7.1	13.9	2.0
Myanmar	—	—	—	3.6	6.7	1.9	—	—	—
PRC	—	—	—	18.4	33.7	1.9	—	—	—
Korea, Republic of	7.7	18.2	2.4	18.8	33.3	1.8	25.8	35.2	1.4
Malaysia	—	—	—	1.6	2.9	1.8	—	—	—
Sri Lanka	1.4	1.7	1.2	2.0	3.6	1.8	—	—	—
Vanuatu	—	—	—	2.0	3.0	1.5	—	—	—
Taipei,China	—	—	—	22.2	30.0	1.4	—	—	—
Thailand	2.7	7.4	3.0	4.9	6.8	1.4	—	—	—
Hong Kong, China	17.5	29.1	1.6	20.9	25.7	1.2	—	—	—
Philippines	5.0	8.0	1.6	16.5	19.8	1.2	—	—	—
Singapore	—	—	—	11.5	12.2	1.1	—	—	—
Tonga	—	—	—	2.2	2.5	1.1	—	—	—
Marshall Islands	—	—	—	—	—	—	8.1	23.4	2.9
Mongolia	—	—	—	—	—	—	6.9	8.9	1.3
Viet Nam	—	—	—	—	—	—	4.5	6.9	1.5

— Data not available.

Note: Data refer to population 20 years old and over.

[a] Table is sorted by this column heading.

Source: ADB 1993, 149-51.

Table A1.2: Political and Economic Participation of Women in DMCs

Economy	Seats in parliament held by women 1999		Female administrators & managers 1992-1996[a]		Female professional & technical workers 1992-1996[a]		Female sales & service workers 1992-1996[a]		Female clerical workers 1992-1996[a]	
	F%	M/F	F%	M/F	F%	M/F	F%	M/F	F%	M/F
Low										
Afghanistan	—	—	—	—	—	—	—	—	—	—
Bangladesh	9.1	10.0	5	19.0	23	3.3	4	24.0	46	1.2
Bhutan	2.0	49.0	—	—	—	—	—	—	—	—
Lao PDR	21.2	3.7	—	—	—	—	—	—	—	—
Nepal	4.5	21.2	—	—	—	—	—	—	—	—
Medium										
Cambodia	8.2	11.2	—	—	—	—	—	—	—	—
PRC	21.8	3.6	12	7.3	45	1.2	52	0.9	39	1.6
Fiji Islands	5.8	16.2	10	9.0	45	1.2	28	2.6	45	1.2
India	8.3	11.0	2	49.0	21	3.8	—	—	—	—
Indonesia	11.4	7.8	7	13.3	41	1.4	58[b]	0.7	44[c]	1.3
Kazakhstan	11.4	7.8	—	—	—	—	—	—	—	—
Kyrgyz Republic	4.8	19.8	—	—	—	—	—	—	—	—
Malaysia	10.3	8.7	19	4.3	44	1.3	40	1.5	54	0.9
Maldives	6.3	14.9	14	6.1	35	1.9	12[b]	7.3	25[c]	3.0
Mongolia	7.9	11.7	—	—	—	—	—	—	—	—
Myanmar	0	all male	—	—	—	—	—	—	—	—
Pakistan	2.0	49.0	4	24.0	20	4.0	5	19.0	2	49.0
Papua New Guinea	1.8	54.6	12	7.3	30	2.3	—	—	—	—
Philippines	12.9	6.8	33	2.0	64	0.6	63	0.6	57	0.8
Samoa	4.1	23.4	12	7.3	47	1.1	54[b]	0.9	53[b]	0.9
Solomon Islands	2.0	49.0	3	32.3	27	2.7	40	1.5	27	2.7
Sri Lanka	5.3	17.9	16	5.3	19	4.3	—	—	44	1.3
Tajikistan	2.8	34.7	—	—	—	—	—	—	—	—
Thailand	6.6	14.2	22	3.5	52	0.9	59	0.7	52	0.9
Uzbekistan	6.0	15.7	13	6.7	35	1.9	—	—	—	—
Vanuatu	0	all male	13	6.7	—	—	—	—	—	—
Viet Nam	26.2	2.8	—	—	—	—	—	—	—	—
High										
Hong Kong, China	—	—	20	4.0	38	1.6	39	1.6	71	0.4
Korea, Republic of	3.7	26.0	4	24.0	32	2.1	60	0.7	52	0.9
Singapore	4.8	19.8	15	5.7	37	1.7	43	1.3	77	0.3

— Data not available.

[a] Data refer to the latest available year in this column heading.

[b] Data exclude sales workers.

[c] Data include sales workers.

Sources: UNDP 1998, 154-5, 188; 1999, 142-5.

Table A1.3: Wages by Occupation and Gender in Lao PDR, 1992 and 1994

	1992			1994		
Occupation	Female	Male	Male/ Female	Female	Male	Male/ Female
Administrator/Manager	19,912	36,712	1.8	37,213	73,522	2.0
Professional/Scientific worker	18,278	24,177	1.3	42,257	53,760	1.3
Technician	13,976	21,649	1.5	36,164	48,328	1.3
Clerk	24,403	27,931	1.1	40,103	48,304	1.2
Service worker	23,777	39,504	1.7	57,709	57,419	1.0
Farm worker	22,794	22,562	1.0	41,098	45,161	1.1
Craft & related trades/Skilled worker	22,219	35,089	1.6	40,309	54,133	1.3
Semi-skilled worker	18,384	29,713	1.6	—	—	—
Unskilled worker	27,193	32,249	1.2	—	—	—
Plant & machine operator	—	—	—	34,255	46,335	1.4
Elementary occupation	—	—	—	31,121	50,645	1.6
Armed forces	—	—	—	41,118	42,256	1.0
Not stated	—	—	—	36,454	39,021	1.1
Average	21,414	29,623	1.4	38,387	50,046	1.3

Source: Netherlands Economic Institute 1995, 28, 75.

Table A1.4: Wages by Level of Education and Gender in Lao PDR, 1992

Level of education	Female	Male	Male/Female
Less than primary	21,760	29,974	1.4
Primary	23,575	32,233	1.4
Lower secondary	19,500	29,672	1.5
Upper secondary	22,193	26,781	1.2
Technical college	17,852	24,363	1.4
Institute	22,271	36,416	1.6
University	24,312	31,025	1.3
Average	21,414	29,623	1.4

Source: Netherlands Economic Institute 1995, 30.

Table A1.5: GDI and GEM Ranks, Combined GER, and Earned Income Share by Gender in DMCs

Economy	GDI Rank 1997[a]	GEM Rank 1997	Combined primary, secondary & tertiary GER 1997			Earned income share 1995		
			M%	F%	M/F	M%	F%	M/F
Low								
Bangladesh	123	83	40	30	1.3	76.9	23.1	3.3
Nepal	121	—	69	49	1.4	66.6	33.4	2.0
Bhutan	119	—	14	10	1.4	67.7	32.3	2.1
Lao PDR	115	—	62	48	1.3	60.4	39.6	1.5
Afghanistan	—	—	—	—	—	—	—	—
Medium								
Pakistan	116	101	56	28	2.0	79.4	20.6	3.9
India	112	95	62	47	1.3	74.6	25.4	2.9
Papua New Guinea	107	91	40	33	1.2	65.1	34.9	1.9
Myanmar	104	—	55	64	0.9	57.7	42.3	1.4
Mongolia	99	—	49	61	0.8	60.3	39.7	1.5
Tajikistan	92	—	73	65	1.1	63.4	36.6	1.7
Viet Nam	91	—	64	59	1.1	58.0	42.0	1.4
Indonesia	88	71	68	61	1.1	67.0	33.0	2.0
PRC	79	40	71	67	1.1	61.9	38.1	1.6
Maldives	77	76	74	75	1.0	64.7	35.3	1.8
Sri Lanka	76	80	65	67	1.0	64.5	35.5	1.8
Philippines	65	45	80	85	0.9	65.0	35.0	1.9
Kazakhstan	64	—	74	79	0.9	60.7	39.3	1.5
Fiji Islands	60	79	81	79	1.0	78.0	22.0	3.5
Thailand	58	64	58	59	1.0	63.3	36.7	1.7
Malaysia	52	52	64	66	1.0	69.6	30.4	2.3
Cambodia	—	—	68	54	1.3	54.8	45.2	1.2
Solomon Islands	—	—	48	44	1.1	60.6	39.4	1.5
Vanuatu	—	—	49	44	1.1	—	—	—
Kyrgyz Republic	—	—	68	71	1.0	60.4	39.6	1.5
Uzbekistan	—	—	78	74	1.1	60.9	39.1	1.6
Samoa	—	—	65	67	1.0	—	—	—
High								
Korea, Republic of	30	78	94	84	1.1	70.8	29.2	2.4
Hong Kong, China	24	—	64	67	1.0	74.4	25.6	2.9
Singapore	22	32	74	71	1.0	68.1	31.9	2.1

— Data not available.
GDI = Gender-related Development Index.
GEM = Gender Empowerment Measure.
GER = gross enrollment rate.
[a] Table is sorted by this column heading.

Sources: UNDP 1998, 131-3; 1999, 138-45, 257.

Table A1.6: Working Population by Education Attainment, Gender and Monthly Wages from Main Employment in Hong Kong, China, 1991

Level of education	a M/F	b M/F	c M/F	d M/F	e M/F	f M/F	g M/F	h M/F	i M/F	j M/F	k M/F
No schooling/kindergarten	0.8	0.3	0.6	2.0	7.1	7.1	3.6	3.6	3.1	3.8	0.2
Primary	1.4	0.6	1.0	2.5	12.3	16.1	12.1	8.8	8.5	7.8	0.2
Lower secondary	2.0	0.9	1.0	2.5	10.0	13.0	10.6	11.1	8.6	5.5	0.4
Upper secondary	1.3	0.8	0.6	0.9	1.5	2.1	2.4	3.0	4.4	5.2	0.4
Matriculation	1.3	1.0	0.4	1.0	1.2	1.3	1.7	2.2	3.7	6.5	0.5
Tertiary: Nondegree	1.1	0.9	0.6	1.0	1.3	1.3	1.3	1.7	2.9	6.2	0.4
Tertiary: Degree	1.7	0.9	0.3	1.7	2.0	2.0	1.9	2.3	2.8	5.3	0.6

a = under HK$1,000; b = HK$1,000-HK$1,999; c = HK$2,000-HK$3,999; d = HK$4,000-HK$5,999; e = HK$6,000-HK$7,999; f = HK$8,000-HK$9,999; g = HK$10,000-HK$14,999; h = HK$15,000-HK$19,999; i = HK$20,000-HK$29,999; j = HK$30,000 and over; k = Unpaid family workers.

Source: Westwood, Mehrain, and Cheung 1995, 88.

Table A1.7: Impact of Additional Schooling on Earnings by Level of Education and Gender in Indonesia, 1986 and 1993

Level of education	1986			1993		
	F%	M%	F/M	F%	M%	F/M
Incomplete primary	2.8	2.8	1.0	2.8	3.9	0.7
Complete primary	3.6	3.6	1.0	3.9	3.7	1.1
Junior high school: General	6.3	4.1	1.5	7.1	4.9	1.4
Junior high school: Vocational	5.7	4.6	1.2	9.4	4.9	1.9
Senior high school: General	9.1	4.7	1.9	10.1	4.3	2.3
Senior high school: Vocational	9.3	4.7	2.0	11.7	5.2	2.3
Diploma I/II	8.9	4.7	1.9	9.7	5.8	1.7
Diploma III	8.9	6.1	1.5	10.7	6.3	1.7
University	9.7	6.9	1.4	10.8	6.5	1.7

Source: World Bank 1996b, 74.

Table A1.8: Women's Political Participation in DMCs, 1996
(percent)

	Women in government		
Economy	*At all levels*	*At ministerial level*	*At subministerial level*
Bangladesh	1.9	7.7	0
Bhutan	5.3	12.5	0
Cambodia	2.4	0	3.1
China, People's Republic of	4.3	6.1	3.9
Fiji Islands	14.5	4.8	18.2
Hong Kong, China	—	—	—
India	4.9	4.8	5.0
Indonesia	1.9	3.6	1.6
Kazakhstan	2.1	2.6	1.7
Korea, Republic of	1.0	3.0	0.6
Kyrgyz Republic	11.4	10.5	12.0
Lao People's Democratic Republic	3.7	0	6.4
Malaysia	8.1	6.1	9.0
Maldives	13.0	5.6	14.1
Mongolia	1.7	0	2.6
Myanmar	0	0	0
Nepal	0	0	0
Pakistan	2.6	4.0	2.2
Papua New Guinea	4.3	0	7.0
Philippines	22.8	4.5	25.3
Samoa	9.1	7.7	9.5
Singapore	7.2	0	9.6
Solomon Islands	0	0	0
Sri Lanka	10.2	13.0	9.6
Tajikistan	3.8	3.7	3.9
Thailand	2.1	0	2.6
Uzbekistan	1.3	2.6	0
Vanuatu	0	0	0
Viet Nam	5.3	7.0	4.4

— Data not available.

Source: UNDP 1999, 238-41.

Table A1.9: Gross Enrollment Rates and Public Education Expenditures in DMCs, 1996
(percent)

	Gross enrollment rates			Public education expenditure		
				Primary & Secondary (as % of all levels)[a]	Higher (as % of all levels)[a]	As % of GNP[a]
Economy	Preprimary	Primary	Secondary	Tertiary		
Low						
Afghanistan	1.0	51.7	21.9	1.7	—	—	—
Bangladesh	75.1	83.8	18.8	6.2	88.6	7.9	2.9
Bhutan	—	—	—	0.2	—	—	—
Lao PDR	7.5	110.7	29.4	2.8	78.0	7.9	2.5
Nepal	1.2	105.1	37.4	4.7	70.2	17.9	3.1
Medium						
Cambodia	5.0	109.2	27.6	1.3	—	—	2.9
PRC	28.9	120.4	70.7	5.7	68.3	15.6	2.3
Fiji Islands	19.0	136.8	69.5	13.1	—	—	—
India	5.3	100.6	49.3	6.9	66.0	13.7	3.4
Indonesia	19.8	114.6	51.8	11.3	72.9	25.1	1.4
Kazakhstan	29.9	95.6	84.6	32.3	60.4	12.5	4.7
Kyrgyz Republic	7.6	108.3	79.7	12.2	68.0	14.1	5.7
Malaysia	58.7	90.9	61.7	11.4	76.3	16.8	5.2
Maldives	60.9	131.0	62.6	—	98.6	—	6.4
Mongolia	24.5	88.7	56.2	17.0	56.0	14.3	6.4
Myanmar	—	99.9	35.4	6.0	88.0	11.7	1.2
Pakistan	15.6	80.7	29.9	3.5	77.3	13.2	3.0
Papua New Guinea	1.3	79.2	13.9	3.2	—	—	—
Philippines	11.3	117.5	79.1	35.2			2.2
Samoa	37.0	102.2	62.4	4.6	—	—	—
Solomon Islands	33.8	98.0	17.9	—	—	—	—
Sri Lanka	60.0	109.1	74.6	5.2	74.8	9.3	3.4
Tajikistan	9.9	93.2	76.2	19.9	71.2	7.1	2.2
Thailand	63.1	88.0	57.0	20.9	73.2	19.4	4.1
Uzbekistan	51.2	79.3	93.0[b]	36.1	69.9	9.7	8.1
Vanuatu	36.7	104.7	21.0[b]	—	90.9	6.4	4.9
Viet Nam	36.3	115.1	40.6[b]	4.7	—	—	2.7
High						
Hong Kong, China	84.8	97.1	74.9	28.0	56.4	37.1	2.9
Korea, Republic of	88.5	94.0	101.8	60.3	81.1	8.0	3.7
Singapore	18.7	94.2	72.5	38.5	60.3	34.8	3.0

— Data not available.
[a] Data refer to the most recent year available.
[b] Data refer to 1994 for Viet Nam; and 1995 for Uzbekistan and Vanuatu.

Sources: ADB 1999, 248; UNDP 1999, 176-9, 257; UNESCO, Division of Statistics 1999.

Table A1.10: Gross Enrollment Rate by Level of Education and Gender in DMCs, 1996

Economy	Primary			Secondary			Tertiary		
	M%	*F%*	*M/F*	*M%*	*F%*	*M/F*	*M%*	*F%*	*M/F*
Low									
Afghanistan	68.4	34.1	2.0	31.8	11.4	2.8	2.4	1.1	2.2
Bangladesh	89.6	77.7	1.2	24.0	13.1	1.8	10.3	1.9	5.4
Bhutan	—	—	—	—	—	—	—	—	—
Lao PDR	122.7	100.6	1.2	36.3	22.7	1.6	3.9	1.6	2.4
Nepal	128.8	95.9	1.3	48.7	25.1	1.9	6.9	2.3	3.0
Medium									
Cambodia	119.4	99.6	1.2	34.7	20.3	1.7	2.1	0.4	5.3
PRC	120.0	119.6	1.0	74.2	66.9	1.1	7.3	3.9	1.9
Fiji Islands	137.2	136.3	1.0	69.4	69.6	1.0	16.1	9.9	1.6
India	109.1	89.7	1.2	58.7	39.2	1.5	8.4	5.2	1.6
Indonesia	114.9	110.4	1.0	55.8	47.6	1.2	14.5	8.0	1.8
Kazakhstan	97.4	98.1	1.0	80.3	88.9	0.9	28.4	36.2	0.8
Kyrgyz Republic	110.1	106.5	1.0	88.9	70.4	1.3	11.6	12.8	0.9
Malaysia	102.8	103.3	1.0	57.5	66.1	0.9	12.6	10.0	1.3
Maldives	133.1	129.8	1.0	60.4	64.9	0.9	—	—	—
Mongolia	86.3	90.7	1.0	47.5	65.0	0.7	10.4	23.8	0.4
Myanmar	92.2	98.1	0.9	34.8	35.9	1.0	4.6	7.4	0.6
Pakistan	109.2	51.0	2.1	38.4	21.0	1.8	4.4	2.6	1.7
Papua New Guinea	85.3	72.9	1.2	16.4	11.2	1.5	4.2	2.1	2.0
Philippines	116.4	118.7	1.0	78.1	80.2	1.0	29.8	40.7	0.7
Samoa	101.3	99.3	1.0	59.4	65.8	0.9	4.7	4.3	1.1
Solomon Islands	102.4	93.4	1.1	21.6	14.0	1.5	—	—	—
Sri Lanka	110.4	108.4	1.0	71.2	78.1	0.9	6.1	4.4	1.4
Tajikistan	96.5	93.8	1.0	80.6	71.7	1.1	26.7	13.0	2.1
Thailand	88.2	87.9	1.0	57.5	56.5	1.0	19.5	22.3	0.9
Uzbekistan	80.4	78.2	1.0	98.4	87.6	1.1	34.0	38.1	0.9
Vanuatu	105.3	104.2	1.0	23.0	19.0	1.2	—	—	—
Viet Nam	117.7	112.3	1.0	41.4	39.7	1.0	6.4	3.0	2.1
High									
Hong Kong, China	96.2	98.1	1.0	72.8	77.3	0.9	30.2	25.5	1.2
Korea, Republic of	93.6	94.4	1.0	101.6	102.0	1.0	73.8	46.0	1.6
Singapore	95.4	93.0	1.0	71.6	73.5	1.0	41.5	35.3	1.2

— Data not available.

Source: UNESCO, Division of Statistics 1999.

Table A1.11: Rural Population, Labor Force, and Adult Illiteracy Rates in DMCs

Economy	Population 1997			GDP share of agriculture 1997 (%)	Labour force (%) Agriculture		Industry		Adult illiteracy rates estimate 1995[b]			
	U%[a]	R%[a]	U/R		1970	1990	1970	1990	Total	M%	F%	M/F
Low												
Afghanistan	21	79	0.3	—	—	—	—	—	68.5	52.8	85.0	1.6
Bangladesh	19	81	0.2	24	84	65	7	16	61.9	50.6	73.9	1.5
Bhutan	7	93	0.1	38	95	94	2	1	57.8	43.8	71.9	1.6
Lao PDR	22	78	0.3	52	81	78	5	6	43.4	30.6	55.6	1.8
Nepal	15	85	0.2	41	94	94	1	0	72.5	59.1	86.0	1.5
Medium												
Cambodia	22	78	0.3	51	79	74	4	8	—	—	—	—
PRC	32	68	0.5	19	78	72	10	15	18.5	10.1	27.3	2.7
Fiji Islands	42	58	0.7	18	52	46	17	15	8.4	6.2	10.7	1.7
India	28	72	0.4	25	73	64	12	16	48.0	34.5	62.3	1.8
Indonesia	37	63	0.6	16	66	55	10	14	16.2	10.4	22.0	2.1
Kazakhstan	61	39	1.6	12	24[c]	22	32[c]	32	—	—	—	—
Kyrgyz Republic	40	60	0.7	45	34[c]	32	29[c]	27	—	—	—	—
Malaysia	55	45	1.2	12	54	27	14	23	16.5	10.9	21.9	2.0
Maldives	27	73	0.4	—	66	32	20	31	—	7	7	1.0
Mongolia	62	38	1.6	37	48	32	21	23	17.1	11.4	22.8	2.0
Myanmar	27	73	0.4	59	78	73	7	10	16.9	11.3	22.3	2.0
Pakistan	36	64	0.6	25	65	52	16	19	—	—	—	—
Papua New Guinea	17	83	0.2	28	82[c]	79	6[c]	7	27.8	19.0	37.3	2.0
Philippines	56	44	1.3	19	58	46	15	15	5.4	5.0	5.7	1.1
Samoa	21	79	0.3	—	—	—	—	—	—	—	—	—
Solomon Islands	18	82	0.2	—	82	77	5	7	—	—	—	—
Sri Lanka	23	77	0.3	22	55	49	14	21	9.8	6.6	12.8	1.9
Tajikistan	32	68	0.5	—	—	41	—	23	—	—	—	—
Thailand	21	79	0.3	11	80[c]	64	6[c]	14	6.2	4.0	8.4	2.1
Uzbekistan	42	58	0.7	31	38[c]	35	25[c]	25	0.3	0.2	0.4	2.0
Vanuatu	20	80	0.3	25	—	—	—	—	—	—	—	—
Viet Nam	21	79	0.3	26	77	71	7	14	6.3	3.5	8.8	2.5
High												
Korea, Rep. of	83	17	4.9 19.	6	49	18	20	35	2.0	0.7	3.3	4.7
Hong Kong, China	95	5	0	0	4	1	55	37	7.8	4.0	11.8	3.0
Singapore	100	0	all urban	0	3	0	30	36	8.9	4.1	13.7	3.3

— Data not available.
U = Urban, R = Rural; M = Male, F = Female.
[a] Data refer to percentage of total.
[b] Data relate to population 15 years old and over.
[c] Data refer to 1980 for Kazakhstan, Kyrgyz Republic, Papua New Guinea, Thailand, and Uzbekistan.

Sources: UNDP 1997,164-5,194,210; 1998, 164-5, 191; 1999, 184-7; World Bank 1999, 28-30.

Table A1.12: Participation of Women in the Teaching Profession in DMCs, 1996

Economy	Primary			Secondary			Tertiary		
	M%[a]	F%[a]	F/M	M%[a]	F%[a]	F/M	M%[a]	F%[a]	F/M
Low									
Afghanistan	—	—	—	—	—	—	—	—	—
Bangladesh	—	—	—	—	—	—	—	—	—
Bhutan	—	—	—	—	—	—	—	—	—
Lao PDR	70	30	0.4	62	38	0.6	71	29	0.4
Nepal	90	10	0.1	—	—	—	—	—	—
Medium									
Cambodia	64	36	0.6	73	27	0.4	83	17	0.2
China, People's Republic of	53	47	0.9	64	36	0.6	70	30	0.4
Fiji Islands	—	—	—	—	—	—	—	—	—
India	74	26	0.4	—	—	—	—	—	—
Indonesia	67	33	0.5	63	37	0.6		—	
Kazakhstan	—	—	—	—	—	—	—	—	—
Kyrgyz Republic	12	88	7.3	33	67	2.0	—	—	—
Malaysia	56	44	0.8	40	60	1.5	—	—	—
Maldives	—	—	—	—	—	—	—	—	—
Mongolia	13	87	6.7	34	66	1.9	64	36	0.6
Myanmar	46	54	1.2	27	73	2.7		—	
Pakistan	68	32	0.5	—	—	—	—	—	—
Papua New Guinea	73	27	0.4	—	—	—			
Philippines	20	80	4.0		—			—	
Samoa	—	—	—	—	—	—	—	—	—
Solomon Islands	—	—	—	—	—	—	—	—	—
Sri Lanka	4	96	24.0	38	62	1.6	66	34	0.5
Tajikistan	46	54	1.2	—	—	—	—	—	—
Thailand	—	—	—	—	—	—	—	—	—
Uzbekistan	18	82	4.6	—	—	—	—	—	—
Vanuatu	—	—	—	—	—	—	—	—	—
Viet Nam	—	—	—	—	—	—	—	—	—
High									
Hong Kong, China	24	76	3.2	50	50	1.0	75	25	0.3
Korea, Republic of	63	37	0.6	61	39	0.6	76	24	0.3
Singapore	23	77	3.3	—	—	—	69	31	0.4

— Data not available.
Note: Data include full-time and part-time teachers.
[a] Data refer to percentage of total.

Source: World Bank 1999, 86-8.

Appendix 2: Country Studies

The following is a list of the eight Country Sector Studies referred to in this booklet:

China, People's Republic of:
National Center for Education Development Research. 1997. *Regional Study of Trends, Issues and Policies in Education: Final Report of Country Case Study of the People's Republic of China.* Country Sector Study prepared for ADB.

Indonesia:
Office of Educational and Cultural Research and Development. 1997. *Study of Trends, Issues and Policies in Education (Indonesia Case Study).* Country Sector Study prepared for ADB. Members of the Research Team included: Sri Hardjoko Wirjomartono (Coordinator); Jiyono; Ace Suryadi; Jahja Umar; Jamil Ibrahim; Arief Sukadi; Suheru Muljoatmodjo; Bambang Indriyanto; Agung Purwadi; Ade Cahyana; Safrudin Chamidi

Kyrgyz Republic:
Kyrgyz Research Institute of Higher Education Problems, Ministry of Education, Science and Culture. Bishkek, Kyrgyz Republic. 1997. *Country Report: Regional Study of Trends, Issues and Policies in Education.* Country Sector Study prepared for ADB. Members of the Research Team included: D.A. Amanaliev; I.B. Becboev; G.M. Belaya; U.N. Brimkulov; N.N. Janaeva; M.T. Imankulova; L.P. Miroshnichenko; V.L. Machnovsky; S.K. Marzaev; A.A. Shaimergenov; V.K. Jantzen.

Nepal:
Research Centre for Educational Innovation and Development, Tribhuvan University. 1997. *Trends, Issues and Policies of Education in Nepal: A Case Study.* Tripureshwor, Kathmandu. Country Sector Study prepared for ADB. Members of the Research Team included: Hridaya Ratna Bajracharya; Bijaya Kumar Thapa; Roshan Chitrakar.

Pakistan:
Pakistan Institute of Development Economics. 1997. *Trends, Issues and Policies in Education: A Case Study of Pakistan.* Islamabad, Pakistan. Country Sector Study prepared for ADB. Researcher: Naushin Mahmood.

Papua New Guinea:

Institute of National Affairs. 1997. *Regional Study of Trends, Issues and Policies in Education: Papua New Guinea Country Case Study.* Country Sector Study prepared for ADB.

Philippines:

Development Academy of the Philippines. 1997. *Policies, Trends and Issues in Philippine Education.* A Case Study Commissioned by UNESCO-Bangkok, Thailand for ADB. The Task Force Members included: Ramon C. Bacani; Napoleon B. Imperial; Juan M. Sabulao; Mario Taguiwalo; Charles C. Villaneuva; Carmencita T. Abella; Alma Bella Z. Generao. Research Team Members included: Elizabeth Y. Manugue - Research Lead; Eduardo T. Gonzalez; Anicetas C. Laquian; Merialda F. Nadunop; Mercedita C. Amar; Shiela D. Valencia.

Viet Nam:

National Institute for Educational Development. 1997. *Regional Study of Trends, Issues and Policies in Education: Viet Nam Case Study.* Hanoi, Viet Nam. Country Sector Study prepared for ADB.

Index